D0911141

SEX ROLE

SOCIALIZATION

A Focus on Women

Lenore J. Weitzman

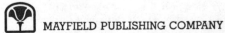 MAYFIELD PUBLISHING COMPANY

LIBRARY OF
WITHDRAWN
EMMITSBURG, MARYLAND

*To my father in celebration of his great love
for his family, his concern for his patients,
and his compassion for humanity*

Copyright © 1979 by Lenore J. Weitzman
First Edition 1979

All rights reserved. No portion of this book may be
reproduced in any form or by any means without
written permission of the publisher.

Library of Congress Catalog Card Number: 78-78142
International Standard Book Number: 0-87484-492-4

Manufactured in the United States of America
Mayfield Publishing Company
285 Hamilton Avenue, Palo Alto, California 94301

This book was set in IBM Aldine Roman by TypArt and was
printed and bound by the George Banta Company.
Sponsoring editor was Alden C. Paine, and Carole Norton
was both managing and manuscript editor. Design by
Nancy Sears and production supervised by Michelle Hogan.
Cover drawing by Maria Jensen.

Contents

v   Preface

ix   Introduction

1   Chapter 1
Early childhood socialization

23   Chapter 2
Variation in sex role standards and behavior

35   Chapter 3
The school years

48   Chapter 4
Socialization pressures in college

67   Chapter 5
The interaction of socialization influences:
The case of mathematics

75   Chapter 6
The achievers: where does socialization fail?

87   Notes

101   Index

Preface

Recent years have brought an explosion of interest in sex roles and a new awareness of the extent to which we have been socialized to become the men and women we are today. Yet much of the important research and writing on sex role socialization has been published in specialized academic journals that are addressed to members of a single discipline and written in highly technical language. As a result, the most recent research is often accessible only to the committed professional—and even the committed professional is likely to have some difficulty keeping up with the rapidly growing literature in both sociology and psychology.

It is my hope that this book will fill the need for a scholarly but readable overview of current work on sex role socialization. It also attempts to provide a critical guide to this work, and to highlight the unresolved questions that remain for future research.

With these very broad aims this book is addressed to a wide variety of audiences: to the reader who wants to understand the forces that have shaped him or her as a man or a woman; to the college student who wants to go beyond the brief treatment of sex role socialization in introductory psychology or sociology; to the graduate student who is searching for a dissertation topic on the cutting edge of the field; and to the professor who is seeking a critical overview of the current state of knowledge.

On a more practical level this book may also be helpful to people who are interested in change—to girls who are trying to understand and resist pressures to conform to sex role stereotypes; to women who want to overcome some of their early socialization; to parents who are trying to raise their children in non-stereotyped ways; to teachers and guidance counselors who are concerned about the unconscious messages that boys and girls receive; and to administrators and employers who are seeking help in planning recruitment and training programs for women.

This book began with an invitation to write a chapter on sex role socialization for Jo Freeman's book, *Women: A Feminist Perspective.* Jo Freeman's detailed critique of my first drafts of this material (for both the first and second editions of her book) were most helpful, and I have benefited greatly from the numerous (and continuous) arguments she has given me over the past eight years. She has been a hard taskmaster, but the process has much improved the material in this book.

I am also indebted to Sheila Tobias and Carol Jacklin for their very different style of collegial support. They each read the final manuscript and offered many thoughtful comments and helpful suggestions. Ruth B. Dixon, Ann E. Freedman, and Sheryl Ruzeck contributed similarly thoughtful comments on earlier drafts, and my research assistants, Susan Feller, Diana Kirk, Peggy Bernardy, and Kyra Subbotin, provided other essential help. This book was written while I was a National Fellow at the Hoover Institution at Stanford University and I am thankful for the institution's support.

My major intellectual debts are to Professors Rose K. Goldsen and William J. Goode. I first studied with Professor Goldsen when I was an undergraduate at Cornell University. Her constant challenges throughout my student years were a continuous source of motivation. I am still grateful to have had a professional role model with such enormous energy and enthusiasm for the research enterprise.

Professor William J. Goode, my dissertation adviser at Columbia, has similarly been a continued inspiration and intellectual role model in his rigorous scholarship, intellectual curiosity, and never-ending quest for knowledge. I am also thankful for his extensive comments on (and his extensive objections to) earlier drafts of this book, as well as for his encouragement and support in my struggle to complete it.

Finally, I would like to thank my intellectual support group, the Berkeley faculty women's research group, for their warm colleagueship over the past three years. While they have not contributed directly to this book, they have contributed a great deal to my life and to my thinking, and I want to express my gratitude to each of them: Carol Bruch, Nancy Chodorow, Ruth Dixon, Fran Flanagan, Susan Ervin-Tripp, Barbara Heyns, Arlie Hochschild, Gertrude Jaeger, Gail Lapidus, Flo Livson, Dale Marshall, Marcia Millman, Karen Paige, Ruth Rosen, Lillian Rubin, Marge Schultz, Arlene Skolnick, Clair Vickery, Norma Wikler, Barbara Zolath, Cynthia Brantley.

Introduction

In our society, women are likely to be characterized as dependent and emotional while men are likely to be considered aggressive, active, and instrumental. How can these differences be explained? Are women "naturally" more dependent, or are they taught to behave that way? Are men inherently more aggressive, or does our society socialize men into more aggressive roles?

To shed some light on the continued controversy over whether (or to what degree) these observed differences are learned or inherent, this book examines the socialization process. It explores the multitude of influences by which the socialization process shapes the roles that most women and men come to accept as entirely natural.

But first, let us consider two important types of data which suggest that studying socialization will help us to understand sex roles today: data on the cross-cultural variation in sex roles, and data on children with biologically ambiguous sexual identities.

Anthropologists who have examined sex roles cross-culturally have found great diversity in the roles assumed "natural" for men and women, and in the extent of differentiation between the sexes. Margaret Mead's classic study of three New Guinea tribes was the first to emphasize this cross-cultural variation in sex roles.[1] In one tribe, the Arapesh, Mead found both men and women who were regarded as cooperative, unaggressive, and responsive to the needs of others—characteristics we would normally label as feminine or maternal. In a second society, the Mundugumor, Mead saw both men and women as aggressive, unresponsive, and individualistic—traits we would normally call masculine. Neither the Arapesh nor the Mundugamor ascribed contrasting personality characteristics to men and women: the Arapesh ideal man, like the ideal woman, was mild and responsive; the Mundugumor ideal for both man and woman was violent and aggressive. In a third (and more controversial) report of yet another society, the Tchambuli, Mead saw a reversal of the typical Western sex roles. The Tchambuli women were dominant, impersonal, and managing; the men were emotionally dependent.

Cross-cultural data such as those collected by Mead are illuminating because they make us realize that some of our basic assumptions about what is "natural" may be based on cultural beliefs rather than on biological necessity. For example, although we have long assumed that women are not fit for war (because they are "naturally" weaker and less aggressive than men), women in other societies, such as the Dahomey in Africa, have been great warriors.* Similarly, we have traditionally regarded women as flirtatious and seductive, but in parts of New Guinea "men are like Victorian women, they are at once prudish and flirtatious, fearful of sex yet preoccupied with love magic and cosmetics that will lead the maidens—who take the initiative in courtship—to be interested in them."[2]

The varied sex role assignments given to men and women in

*It should be noted, however, that physical strength is almost irrelevant in the modern industrial society. No such society gives its highest rewards of money, power, or prestige on the basis of physical strength.

different cultures suggest that the basic characteristics of men and women are not biologically determined; rather, they are based on cultural definitions of sex-appropriate behavior. Since we have no reason to assume that the biological makeup of men and women in Mead's tribes or in other societies differs from that of men and women in the United States in any basic way, the observed differences between the sexes in these cultures and our own would seem to be culturally determined.*

The compelling logic of this conclusion becomes more obvious when we consider the alternative: if we hypothesize a biological basis for these differences we ought then to conclude that Tchambuli men are dependent because they have more female hormones. This would be akin to concluding that Latin American men are more *macho* than American men because of higher levels of male hormones, or that Oriental women are less aggressive than American women because they have more female hormones.** Since we know there is no such cross-cultural variation in biological or hormonal sex, we must look to the influence of cultural learning to these differences.†

*However, we still have not adequately explained what Professor Michelle Rosaldo refers to as the "striking and surprising fact that male activities are always recognized as predominantly important." Rosaldo points out that even when women have a great deal of power, male activities are typically regarded as more important. This observation is amply supported by the findings of others. For example, among the African Yoruba, Lloyd reports, women "control a good part of the food supply, accumulate cash, and trade in distant and important markets; yet when approaching their husbands, wives must feign ignorance and obedience, kneeling to serve the men as they sit." Similarly, in the Jewish ghetto communities of Eastern Europe, Zborowski and Herzog found that women typically ran the household and the family economy: women worked to provide family support, had more practical knowledge than their husbands, and made most of the economic decisions for the family; but they nevertheless deferred to their husbands. Michelle Zimbalist Rosaldo and Louise Lamphere, eds., *Woman, Culture, and Society* (Stanford, Calif.: Stanford University Press, 1974), pp. 19-20, citing P. C. Lloyd, "The Yoruba of Nigeria," in James L. Gibbs, ed., *Peoples of Africa* (New York, 1965), and Mark Zborowski and Elizabeth Herzog, *Life Is With People* (New York, 1955).

**As the Bems have observed, "If female hormones are responsible for keeping women from high level jobs, we would have to assume that women in the Soviet Union have different hormones, because they comprise 33 percent of the engineers and 75 percent of the doctors." Sandra Bem and Daryl Bem, "Training Woman to Know Her Place: The Power of a Nonconscious Ideology," *Psychology Today,* November 1970.

†The cultural learning theory is supported by Beatrice Whiting's and Carolyn Pope Edwards' cross-cultural study of sex differences in 3-11 year old children. Whiting and Edwards

The power of cultural factors is further suggested by a very different line of research: the work of Money and Ehrhardt and of Hampson and Hampson[3] on hermaphrodites. A hermaphrodite is an individual who possesses a full set of both male and female genitalia and reproductive organs. While a complete hermaphrodite is extremely rare, a fair number of babies are born each year whose sex is difficult to determine with certainty. Some of these infants appear to be female but are biologically male; others appear to be male but are biologically female. Dr. John Money and his associates at Johns Hopkins University have spent almost twenty years following the life histories of some of these babies. Of greatest interest to us here are those babies who were assigned one sex at birth but later found to belong biologically (genetically, gonadally, hormonally) to the opposite sex. In virtually all these cases, the sex of assignment (and thus of rearing) proved dominant. Babies designated males at birth and brought up as boys by their parents (who were unaware of their child's true female genetic and hormonal makeup) thereafter thought of themselves as boys, played with boys' toys, enjoyed boys' sports, preferred boy's clothing, developed male sex fantasies, and in due course fell in love with girls. And the reverse was true for babies who were biologically male but reared as girls: they followed the typical feminine pattern of development—they preferred marriage over a career, enjoyed domestic and homemaking duties, and saw their future fulfillment in the traditional woman's role.

This research dramatically illustrates the impact of socialization —even when it contradicts biological sex—and thus further supports the importance of learned differences as determinants of sex roles. Having indicated the powerful influence of culturally transmitted definitions of sex roles, let us now examine the process by which sex roles are transmitted—the process of socialization.

---

found that many sex differences in children's behavior can be attributed to socialization pressures in the form of task assignments. For example, girls are more likely to be assigned to care for children under 18 months and this contributes to nurturance behavior, i.e., the offering of help and support. However, when boys are similarly required to tend babies they also score higher on offerings of help and support. Whiting and Edwards, "A Cross Cultural Analysis of Sex Differences in the Behavior of Children Aged Three through 11," *The Journal of Social Psychology*, 91 (1973): 171-188.

Sex Role

Socialization

Early

childhood

socialization

Chapter 1

From the minute a newborn baby girl is wrapped in a pink blanket and her brother in a blue one, the two children are treated differently. The difference starts with the subtle tones of voice adults use in cooing over the two cradles, and it continues with the father's mock wrestling with his baby boy and gentler play with his "fragile" daughter.[1]

In one study Rubin, Provenzano, and Luria interviewed the mothers and fathers of newborn infants on the day of the child's birth.[2] The fathers were interviewed almost immediately after the delivery, while the mothers, who were often under sedation at the time of delivery, were interviewed up to but not later than 24 hours

1

later. The fathers were not permitted to handle their babies during the first 24 hours but could view them through display windows in the hospital nursery. Most of the mothers, on the other hand, had held and fed their infants. The parents were asked to describe the baby as they would to a close friend or relative. They also rated the baby on an 18-item bipolar scale, choosing between adjectives such as *noisy* versus *quiet, active* versus *inactive, strong* versus *weak, cheerful* versus *cranky,* and *easy-going* versus *fussy.*

Both parents described daughters, in contrast to sons, as softer, finer featured, weaker, smaller, prettier, more inattentive, more awkward, and more delicate. Sons were characterized as firmer, larger featured, better coordinated, more alert, stronger, and hardier.[3] Although mothers and fathers generally agreed on the sex-differentiated characteristics, the fathers were stronger sex-typers in that they labeled the two sexes farther apart on the adjective pairs. (However, one measure produced a cross-sex effect: mothers rated sons as cuddlier than daughters while fathers rated daughters as cuddlier than sons, a finding the researchers dubbed the "oedipal effect.")

The results of this study are impressive in light of the fact that the sample of newborn male and female babies did not differ in average length, weight, or Apgar scores. Thus the differences the parents perceived in the children seem to be a pure case of parental labeling. Rubin, Provenzano, and Luria conclude that "sex-typing and sex-role socialization appear to have already begun their course at the time of the infant's birth, when information about the infant is minimal, ... [and these labels] may well affect subsequent expectations about the manner in which their infant ought to behave as well as parental behavior itself."[4]

In another innovative study Will, Self, and Datan observed eleven mothers, who each played, in turn, with a six-month-old child.[5] Six of the women were told the child was a boy; the other five were told it was a girl. The researchers then observed which of three toys—a doll, a train, or a fish—the mothers offered the child. Although each mother claimed she did not distinguish between boys and girls at that age, the women who thought the child was a girl most often offered "her" a doll to play with. The women who thought the child was a boy offered "him" a train. In addition, the mothers who thought the child a girl commented that "she was a real girl": "she was sweeter and cried more softly than a boy would."[6] (In fact, the child was a boy.)

Other researchers have observed culturally conventional sex differences in the behavior of children at very young ages, most of it directly traceable to parents' differential treatment of baby boys and girls. For example, Moss observed mothers' treatment of their newborn children at three weeks and three months, and found that the infants were being given consistent reinforcement for sex-appropriate behavior.[7] In fact, Moss tentatively suggests that patterns leading to verbal ability in girls and aggression in boys were being selectively encouraged in the infants he observed.[8]

In observing thirteen-month-old babies, Goldberg and Lewis found that the girls clung to, looked at, and talked to their mothers more often than the boys.[9] Each of these behavioral differences was linked to differential treatment by the mother when the babies were younger. The researchers had observed the same mothers with their babies when the babies were six months old. At that stage they observed that mothers of girl babies touched their infant girls more often then did mothers of infant boys. They also talked to and handled their daughters more often.[10] By the time these same children were thirteen months old, the researchers observed that the girl babies had learned to respond to the more frequent stimuli they received from their mothers: they reciprocated their mothers' attention with the result that by thirteen months they talked to and touched their mothers more often than the boys did. In order to establish the causal relationship, i.e., that high frequency of touching at six months causes babies to seek more touching at thirteen months, Goldberg and Lewis reclassified the mothers they had observed at six months into groups with high and low rates of touching. They found that the children (both boys and girls) of mothers with high touching rates at six months sought the most maternal contact at thirteen months.[11]

This research vividly illustrates socialization at its earliest stages. It indicates that sex role socialization begins before the child is even aware of a sexual identity: before he or she can have an internal motive for conforming to sex role standards. It also indicates that cultural assumptions about what is "natural" for a boy or for a girl are so deeply ingrained that parents may treat their children differentially without even being aware of it. Presumably, if we interviewed mothers of six-month-old babies, they would not tell us that they expected their young sons to be independent and assertive while still in the cradle. Yet, it appears that at some level mothers do have such expectations, and these expectations are successfully communicated to very young babies. Thus, wittingly or unwittingly, parents encourage and reinforce sex-appropriate behavior, and little boys and little girls respond to parental encouragement and rewards. So little boys learn to be independent, active, and aggressive; their sisters learn to be dependent, verbal, and social.

EARLY COGNITIVE SOCIALIZATION

We have been discussing the first type of socialization an infant experiences: simple behavior reinforcement. A second type of socialization begins with cognitive learning—when the child is able to sort out and make conceptual distinctions about the social world and herself or himself. Around the age of three or four, the child begins to make sex role distinctions and express sex role preferences. Rabban found that at the age of three both boys and girls still showed incomplete recognition of sex differences and were unaware of the appropriateness of sex-typed toy objects.[12] Each year, however, children's cognitive abilities increase: by age six they are able to distinguish the male and female role clearly, and to identify themselves appropriately. Sex role learning in these preschool years may be divided into three analytic processes. The child learns:

1. to *distinguish* between men and women and between boys and girls, and to know what kinds of behavior are characteristic of each;
2. to express appropriate sex role *preferences* for himself or herself; and
3. to *behave* in accordance with sex role standards.

In labeling these processes I have avoided the term *identification* because of the distinct meaning of this word in the socialization literature. Identification, a frequently used concept in Freudian theory, assumes that sex role learning is limited to the same-sex parent. This theory will be discussed (and criticized) in the final chapter of this book. In the following pages each of these three processes will be discussed separately because each presents a different set of contingencies for the growing boy or girl.

DISTINGUISHING BETWEEN MALE AND FEMALE ROLES

Both boys and girls learn to distinguish the male from the female role by observing the men and women around them: their parents, brothers and sisters, neighbors, and friends. In addition to serving as models for the young child, these adults and older boys and girls often provide explicit instructions on proper behavior.

It is widely believed that parents are especially influential in defining the male and female role for the young child. They do this both consciously and unconsciously, by example and proscription, by reward and punishment. There is some evidence that fathers continue to be more concerned than mothers with sex-typing in young children. Goodenough's interviews with the parents of two- to four-year-old children indicated that fathers more strictly differentiated sex roles and encouraged stronger sex typing in children than did mothers.[13]

Until recently, most researchers simply assumed that parents play the dominant role in teaching sex role stereotypes to children. However, after a comprehensive review of the research literature, Stanford psychologists Eleanor Maccoby and Carol Jacklin concluded that "the research on socialization of the two sexes has revealed surprisingly *little differentiation in parent behavior* according to the sex of the child."[14]

One possible explanation for this finding is that past research has been ill designed to measure the influence of parents. Berkeley psychologist Jeanne Block suggests that the published research reviewed by Maccoby and Jacklin relies on samples that tend to obscure sex differences.[15] For example, Block notes, only 9 percent of the studies focused on fathers. Since fathers are more sex-differentiating this may have biased the results. Moreover, Block points out that 77 percent of the studies cited by Maccoby and Jacklin relate to the socialization of children aged five and younger. In some important areas—in achievement, for instance—sex-related differences in socialization are unlikely to occur at that early age. Indeed, in the minority of studies (23 percent) that deal with children over age six, sex-differential parental behaviors appear more frequently.

Block's own research on parental training, which takes in 17 samples in six countries, revealed that sex-differentiation in socialization increased with the age of the child and peaked during the teen years.[16] Both parents were more likely to train their daughters in traditional feminine behavior than in achievement-related skills. Both "emphasized achievement, competition, independence, and taking personal responsibility more for sons than daughters," and both encouraged "ladylike" behavior in females. Block also found that fathers were more concerned with their daughters' affective and social skills. In teaching their daughters they paid more attention to social factors than to the girl's performance. Other research suggests that girls whose fathers encourage feminine behavior typically display more traditional sex-typed behavior.[17]

A second interpretation of the Maccoby-Jacklin finding is that past research has not adequately measured the great variety of ways in which parents communicate sex-typed expectations. For example, in a recent observational study, psychologist Esther Greif reported that parents differentially interrupt their sons and their daughters.[18] In fact, parents interrupt girls twice as much as they interrupt boys. Greif also found that fathers interrupt children of both sexes more than mothers do. Since interruptions provide a clear index of relative power and importance, children who are frequently interrupted are subtly being told their opinions are not worthy of serious attention. This type of communication is often much more effective than parental assertions that they "treat all their children alike."

A third inference that could be drawn from the Maccoby-Jacklin research is that the overall socialization influence of parents has been exaggerated. Without question, the predisposition of psychologists to concentrate their investigations on family influences in general, and on influences present in the early childhood years in particular, has produced a major bias in the socialization literature. In this book, however, we examine a much broader range of socialization influences. Let us now turn to some of these other influences.

Picture books are another important source of sex role learning for young children. Through books, children learn about the world outside their immediate environment: they learn what other boys and girls do, say, and feel, and they learn what is expected of children of their age. Picture books are especially important to the preschool child because they are often looked at over and over again at a time when children are in the process of developing their own sex role identities. In addition, they are read to children before other socialization influences (such as school, teachers, and peers) become important in their lives.

Weitzman, Eifler, Hokada, and Ross examined the treatment of sex roles in those children's books identified as the "very best": the winners of the coveted Caldecott Medal for the most distinguished picture book of the year.[19] They found that the most salient fact about the image of females in children's books was simply, that they were invisible. Females were underrepresented in titles, central roles, pictures, and stories. Most of the books were about boys, men, and male animals, and most dealt exclusively with male adventures. The Caldecott winners examined had eleven pictures of males for every one picture of a female.[20]

The female characters who did appear were usually insignificant or inconspicuous. For example:

> "There are two women in [the book] *The Fool of the World:*
> the mother, who packs lunch for her sons and waves goodbye,
> and the princess whose hand in marriage is the object of the
> Fool's adventures. The princess is shown only twice . . . .
> She does not have anything to say throughout the adventure,
> and of course she is not consulted in the choice of her husband;
> on the last page, however, the narrator assures us that she soon
> "loved him to distraction." Loving, watching, and helping are
> among the few activities allowed to women in picture books.[21]

Weitzman *et al.* found that the girls in the Caldecott books were typically portrayed as passive and doll-like, while the boys were shown as active and adventuresome. Most of the girls engaged in service activities directed toward pleasing and helping their brothers and fathers. The boys, by contrast, engaged in a variety of tasks requiring independence and self-confidence.

Picture books also provide children with images of what they will be like when they grow up. Boys and girls are likely to identify with adults of the same sex, and to desire to be like them. Thus, adult role models influence a child's aspirations and goals. However, in award-winning picture books Weitzman *et al.* found the adult women role models to be stereotyped and limited:

> Obadiah's mother cooks, feeds him hot chocolate, and goes to church. The wife of the Sun God carries wood to help him build the house, but she never speaks. Sylvester's mother is shown sweeping, packing a picnic lunch, knitting, and crying. And Mrs. Noah, who had an important role in the biblical story of the flood, is completely omitted from the children's book version.[22]

Even the motherhood role is unrealistically proscribed:

> The mother is almost always confined to the house, although she is usually too well dressed for housework. Her duties are not portrayed as difficult or challenging—she is shown as a housebound servant who cares for her husband and children. She washes dishes, cooks, vacuums, yells at the children, cleans up, does the laundry, and takes care of babies. For example, a typical domestic scene in *Sylvester and the Magic Pebble* shows the father reading the paper, Sylvester playing with his rock collection, and the mother sweeping the floor.[23]

As the authors note, the picture books disregard the more imaginative things that real mothers do.[24]

In all the Caldecott winners only one adult female played an active leadership role—a fairy godmother who was clearly not a "normal" woman, but a mythical creature. In contrast, the roles that men played were varied, interesting, and for the most part attainable. They were storekeepers, housebuilders, storytellers, monks, fighters, fishermen, policemen, soldiers, adventurers, fathers, cooks, preachers, judges, and farmers. They were also the kings and the gods. Not one woman in the Caldecott sample had a job or profession;

not one father helped in the mundane duties of child care, dish-washing, cooking, cleaning, or shopping. The authors conclude that in the world of picture books:

> Little girls receive attention and praise for their attractiveness, while boys are admired for their achievements and cleverness. For girls, achievement is marriage and becoming a mother. Most of the women in picture books have status by virtue of their relationships to specific men—they are the wives of the kings, judges, adventurers and explorers, but they themselves are not the rulers, judges, adventurers and explorers.
>
> Through picture books, girls are taught to have low aspirations because there are so few opportunities portrayed as available to them. The world of picture books never tells little girls that as women they might find fulfillment outside of their homes or through intellectual pursuits. . . .
>
> In a country with over 40 percent of the women in the labor force it is absurd to find that women in picture books remain only mothers and wives. . . .
>
> Their future occupational world is presented as consisting primarily of glamour and service. Women are excluded from the world of sports, politics and science. They can achieve only by being attractive, congenial and serving others.[25]

Another much-discussed source of sex role socialization for young children is television. Gardner's study of the program *Sesame Street* (another supposed ideal) suggests that television contributes equally to severe sex role stereotypes:

> On one program, Big Bird (having said that he would like to be a member of a family and having been told that Gordon and Susan would be his family) is told that he will have to help with the work and that since he is a boy bird, he will have to do men's work—the heavy work, the *"important"* work and also that he should get a girl (bird) to help Susan with *her* work of arranging flowers, redecorating, etc. There was more and virtually all of it emphasized that there is men's work and then there is women's work—that men's work is outside the home and women's work is in the home. (This in spite of the fact that 17 *million* children under eighteen have mothers who are employed outside the home; of these, 4.5 million are under six.)[26]

9

More recently Sternglanz and Serbin have analyzed the most popular commercially produced children's television programs.[27] Because they wanted to compare the treatment of males and females in these programs, they limited their sample to programs with at least one male and one female character. This restriction meant they had to eliminate half of the most widely viewed (according to Nielson ratings) programs. Yet even in this less inclusive group of ten popular programs they found that two thirds of the characters were male.

The researchers also observed statistically significant differences in the behaviors of the two sexes. Males were more often portrayed as aggressive and constructive, while females were more likely to be shown as deferent.[28] In addition, males were more likely to be rewarded for their behavior, while females more often received *no reaction.* An exception to this rule was found only when females exhibited high levels of activity; then they were more likely to be *punished.*

As Sternglanz and Serbin note, "there is clear indication that modeling is a powerful technique for influencing children's behavior. Imitative learning appears to occur spontaneously in many situations, and to account for a significant portion of a child's behavioral repertoire."[29] In addition to providing a model for sex-appropriate behavior, these programs provide a powerful lesson in negative modeling: a child who identifies with the female characters learns it is sex-inappropriate for girls to be too active or aggressive, and a child who identifies with the male characters learns it is sex-inappropriate for boys to defer to or express admiration for others.[30]

· Although the images in children's books and TV programs appear to be more stereotyped and rigid than reality, interviews with young children indicate the extent to which these clearly differentiated sex roles are internalized by the child. Hartley asked a sample of young boys what they thought was expected of boys and girls. Her respondents described boys as follows:

> They have to be able to fight in case a bully comes along; they
> have to be athletic; . . . they must be able to play rough
> games . . . they need to be smart; they need to be able to take
> care of themselves; they should know what girls don't know . . .
> they should have more ability than girls . . . they are expected

to get dirty; to mess up the house; to be naughty; to be outside more than girls are; not to be cry babies, not to be softies; and to get into trouble more than girls do.[31]

Girls, according to the boy respondents,

have to stay close to home; they are expected to play quietly and more gently than boys; they are often afraid; they must not be rough; they have to keep clean; they cry when scared or hurt; their activities consist of "fopperies" like playing with dolls, fussing over babies, and sitting and talking about dresses; they need to know how to cook, sew and take care of children, but spelling and arithmetic are not as important for them as for boys.[32]

When Hartley asked her young respondents about adults, she found their images of the two sexes even more disparate. In the children's eyes men are active and intelligent,

strong, ready to make decisions, protect women and children in emergencies. . . . They must be able to fix things, they must get money to support their families, and have a good business head. Men are the boss in the family and have the authority to dispose of money and they get first choice in the use of the most comfortable chair in the house and the daily paper. . . . They laugh and make more jokes than women do. Compared with mothers, fathers are more fun to be with: they are exciting to have around and they have the best ideas.[33]

In contrast, women are seen as a rather tired and unintelligent group.

They are indecisive and they are afraid of many things; they make a fuss over things, they get tired a lot . . . they don't know what to do in an emergency, they cannot do dangerous things, they are scared of getting wet or getting an electric shock, they are not very intelligent. . . . Women do things like cooking and washing and sewing because that's all they can do.[34]

EXPRESSING SEX ROLE PREFERENCES

Once the child has learned to distinguish males from females and has determined the types of behavior that are appropriate for each, he

11

or she may begin to express sex role preferences. Rabban found that both boys and girls at age three decidedly prefer the mother role when asked to choose which parent they would prefer to be like.[35] Other studies have corroborated this preference of young children for the mother.* According to the reasons the children themselves give for their preference, they like best the parent who caters to their material wants, who expresses affection for them, who plays with them most, and who punishes them least.[36]

But the sex role preferences of children soon change. By age five most boys, and a significant minority of girls, say they prefer the masculine role. Brown, interviewing five- and six-year-old children, found more cross-sex preferences among girls (indicating a desire to be boys) than among boys.[37] In addition, the boys show a significantly stronger preference for the masculine role than girls reveal for the feminine role.[38] The research of Hartup and Zook corroborates the finding about strength of preference[39] and indicates, further, that with each year more girls prefer to identify with the masculine role than boys with the feminine role.[40]

One explanation for the general preference for the male role is that both boys and girls have learned it is more prestigious in our society. Thus, it is preferable. Hartley's study, cited above, clearly indicates that children perceive the superior status and privileges of the masculine role.[41] They know which sex gets the best chair in the house, and which sex is expected to do the cleaning.[42] Brown, using the values children give to sex-typed toys, also concluded that the children saw the masculine role as having greater prestige and value.[43] Smith has found evidence to suggest that as children grow older, they increasingly learn to give males more prestige.[44] He asked children from eight to fifteen to vote on whether boys or girls have desirable or undesirable traits. With increasing age both boys and girls increasingly ascribed the desirable traits to boys. In addition, boys expressed a progressively better opinion of themselves while self-conceptions of girls progressively weakened.[45]

Thus children learn that it is better to be a male than a female because it is men who exhibit the highly valued traits and are accorded

*These preferences of young children challenge Freud's theory of penis envy. They suggest, rather, that young boys may experience something akin to breast envy.

the privilege and prestige in our society.* No wonder, then, that girls are reluctant to express "appropriate" sex role preferences, and instead continue wishing they were boys. Boys, by contrast, find it easy to express "appropriate" sex role preferences.

While it is likely that young girls have experienced a considerable amount of role conflict in learning to express "appropriate" sex role preferences in the past, this may now be changing. The women's liberation movement is not only trying to instill a sense of pride in girls, but it is also aiming at changing the structural conditions in our society which have, in the past, made it more desirable to be a male.

LEARNING SEX ROLE BEHAVIOR

The third component of the socialization process consists of learning to act like a girl or a boy.

Boys are said to have more difficulty learning appropriate sex role behavior. Their difficulty stems from three sources: the lack of continuous male role models, the rigidity and harshness of male sex role demands, and the negative nature of male sex role proscriptions.

Several theorists have suggested that boys know less about the masculine role because of the relative lack of salience of the father as a model. Lynn notes that the father is in the home much less than the mother, and even when he is there, he usually participates in fewer intimate activities with the child than the mother does.[46] Both the amount of time spent with the child, and the intimacy and intensity of parental contact are thought to be important for the child's learning. Since the girl is able to observe her mother throughout the day and has continuous and intimate contact with her, she supposedly finds it easier to use her mother as a model, and to imitate appropriate sex role behavior.

Lynn has further theorized that because boys have less direct exposure to male models they tend to develop stereotypical images

*Alice Rossi has suggested that girls get a more subtle message with regard to the relative prestige of men and women. They learn that outside the home men are the bosses of women; however, in the home, father does not know best. The message thus communicated to little girls is that women can be important only in the family. Alice Rossi, "Equality Between the Sexes," in Robert J. Lifton, ed., *The Woman in America* (Boston: Houghton Mifflin, 1964), p. 105.

of masculinity.[47] This view has been supported by studies showing that fatherless boys have more exaggerated notions of what constitutes masculinity than do boys who have a father in the home.[48] The tendency of boys to pattern themselves after a male stereotype may help account for the exaggerated forms of masculinity encouraged by male peer groups. In the absence of fuller role models to emulate, boys may view extremes of "toughness" and aggression as appropriate male behavior.

Hartley has suggested that boys have the additional problem of a more rigorous sex role definition: "Demands that boys conform to social notions of what is manly come much earlier and are enforced with much more vigor than similar attitudes with respect to girls. These demands are frequently enforced harshly, impressing the small boy with the danger of deviating from them, while he does not quite understand what they are."[49] By contrast, very young girls are allowed a wider range of behavior and are punished less severely for deviation, especially in the middle class. (At young ages it is easier for a girl to be a tomboy than for a boy to be a sissy.) Upon reaching adolescence, however, the behavior of girls is more sharply constricted than is boys'.

In addition to the relative absence of male role models and the rigidity of the male sex role, the socialization of boys is said to be characterized by negative proscriptions.[50] Boys are constantly warned *not* to be sissies, and *not* to engage in other feminine behavior. The literature on learning suggests that it is harder to learn from punishment than from rewards, because the desired behavior is not enunciated in the sanction and therefore remains obscure.[51] Thus some theorists have asserted that the socialization of boys is particularly conducive to anxiety. In Hartley's words,

> the child is asked to do something which is not clearly defined for him, based on reasons he cannot possibly appreciate, and enforced with threats, punishments, and anger by those who are close to him. . . . Anxiety frequently expresses itself in over-straining to be masculine, in virtual panic at being caught doing anything traditionally defined as feminine, and in hostility toward anything even hinting at "femininity," including females themselves.[52]

In contrast to the anxiety-producing sex role learning of the boy, the socialization literature characterizes the young girl's experiences as easy. She is supposedly provided with more positive opportunities to learn appropriate role behavior through her frequent interaction with her mother* as well as the chance to try out her feminine role in her doll play.[53]

This idyllic view of the learning process for girls appears naive to any woman who has been socialized in a middle-class family. It is clear that the sex role socialization process is equally anxiety-producing for girls, although for somewhat different reasons. The girl is provided with a female model, and is afforded more opportunity to "play out" the "appropriate" behavior, but the role she is asked to play is clearly not a desirable one. As already noted, children understand the relative worth of the two sexes at quite young ages. The little girl is therefore aware of the fact that she is being pushed, albeit gently, into a set of behaviors that are neither considered desirable nor rewarded by the society at large. For example, she is told that it is feminine to play house: to wash dishes, set the table, dress her doll, vacuum the floor, and cook the dinner. In many middle-class homes these activities are delegated to paid domestics, or performed with obvious distaste. Why, then, should the little girl want to imitate those behaviors? I would hypothesize the little girl becomes quite anxious about being encouraged to perform a series of behaviors that are held in low esteem. I would hypothesize further that she experiences considerable internal conflict when she realizes that her mother, a loved model, receives neither recognition nor satisfaction for such activities, and yet encourages them in her.

In addition to perceiving the low evaluation of feminine activities, many young girls find boys' activities intrinsically more enjoyable. For example, boys' toys allow a much broader range of activity as well as more initiative, creativity, and adventure. One study found that the average price of boys' toys was much greater than

*This statement presumes a family in which the mother stays at home. It ignores the reality in an increasingly significant number of families in which mothers of preschool children work and may thus have no more frequent contact with their children than working fathers do.

that of girls' toys for each age group.[54] More girls in Ward's sample preferred boys' toys than preferred girls' toys.[55] Respondents in Komarovsky's study expressed a similar interest in boys' toys—in chemistry sets, baseball gloves, and electric trains. "One of my biggest disappointments as a child," wrote a girl in Komarovsky's study, "happened one Christmas. I asked for a set of tools . . . only to find a sewing set."[56]

Since most growing children enjoy being active, running and playing outside, getting dirty if necessary, and being allowed to explore their own interests, it is not surprising that many girls prefer "boys'" activities, and resent being restricted to being "a sweet little girl." Komarovsky's students reported that they envied the freedom their brothers and other boys were allowed, and resented being constrained to play with "girls' toys," to be sedentary, quiet, and neat in their play.[57]

In reviewing the socialization literature I was struck by the fact that the harsh restrictions placed on boys are often discussed, but those placed on girls are ignored. In fact, there is no reason to believe that the socialization of boys involves greater restrictiveness, control, and protectiveness.[58] Boys may be punished more often, but girls' activities are likely to be so severely constrained to begin with that they never have a chance to engage in punishable behavior. It is also possible that the kinds of sanctions used to socialize women may be more subtle, but no less severe: boys are spanked, but girls may be made to feel unworthy, deviant, guilty, or queer.[59] The following quotes from Komarovsky's study indicate the powerful sanctions and the resulting anguish experienced by girls whose desires conflict with the sex role preferences of their parents:

> I started life as a little tomboy but as I grew older, Mother got worried about my unladylike ways. She removed my tops, marbles, football, and skates and tried to replace these with dolls, tea sets and sewing games. To interest me in dolls she collected dolls of different nations, dressed exquisitely in their native costumes. . . .
>
> When despite her efforts she caught me one day trying to climb a tree in the park she became thoroughly exasperated and called me a little "freak."

Once I got very dirty playing and Mother told me that if I didn't learn to play quietly and keep myself neat no man would ever want to marry me.

I was a member of a Brownie Troop when I was seven and we were to have a party one day to which each child was to bring her favorite toy. My favorite toy at that time was a set of tin soldiers. Grandmother was shocked and insisted that I would disgrace her by bringing such an unladylike toy. But I refused to take a doll, with the result that I was forced to miss the party. But Grandmother succeeded in making me feel quite "queer" because I didn't like dolls.[60]

These quotes suggest the very real pressures that are brought to bear on the girl whose temperamental preferences do not conform to the feminine stereotype.

In summary, the socialization of boys and of girls may present different sets of difficulties, but difficulties and anxiety in the socialization process are common to both. Typically, girls have more readily available role models, but they probably have less motivation to imitate those models because they (correctly) view the role as more confining and less rewarding than the masculine role. Boys may have less salient role models, and experience more frequent physical punishment, but they have more motivation to learn the masculine role because they (correctly) view it as more highly valued than the feminine, allowing more exciting and interesting activities.

Consequently, socialization must be understood as two very different but equally anxiety-producing processes for boys and girls because it requires them both to conform to rigid sex role standards that are often in conflict with their individual temperaments or preferences. To the extent that we continue to define appropriate sex role behavior for men and women as polar opposites, we will continue to push many individuals into unnatural molds.

THE LEARNING PROCESS: REACTIONS, REWARDS AND PUNISHMENT

Let us now briefly consider how specific characteristics are encouraged in children of each sex. According to Kagan, the typical child seeks the acceptance of parents and peers and wants to avoid their rejection. These motives predispose her or him to shun inappropriate activities, and to choose responses that are congruent with sex role standards.[61]

Parents say that they want their daughters to be passive, nurturing, and dependent and their sons to be aggressive and independent. Therefore, most parents punish aggression in their daughters, directly or indirectly,[62] and passivity and dependency in their sons.[63] For example, the little girl is allowed to cling to her mother's apron, but her brother is told he can't be a "sissy" and must go off on his own. The dependency and affection-seeking responses seen as normal for both boys and girls in early childhood become defined as feminine in older children.[64] The result, as Bardwick has noted, is that girls are not separated from their parents as sources of support and nurturance, and they are therefore not forced to develop internal controls and an independent sense of self.[65] Instead, the self they value is one that emanates from the appraisals of others. Consequently girls develop a greater need for the approval of others and a greater fear of rejection[66] than do boys.

Kagan has observed that our definition of femininity *requires* reactions from other people. The young girl cannot assess whether she is attractive, nurturing, or helpful without continual interaction and feedback from others.[67] She is thus forced to be dependent on people and to court their acceptance in order to obtain those experiences that help to establish sex-typed behaviors.[68]

In contrast, the boy is encouraged to be self-reliant. Many masculine sex-typed behaviors, especially those involving physical skills, can be developed alone. A boy is taught to stand up for himself and engage in certain behavior because he, as a person, feels that it is appropriate. In fact, men who stand by their individual principles despite opposition and the scorn of others often become cultural heroes.

According to Bronfenbrenner, different methods of child training are used for boys than for girls. Boys are subjected to more physical punishment, whereas pyschological punishments, such as the threat of withdrawal of love, are more frequently used for girls.[69] Children trained with physical punishment have been shown to be more self-reliant and independent.[70] The other method of child training—the love oriented psychological method—usually produces children who are more obedient and dependent.[71] As girls are most often trained with psychological methods they are exposed to more affection and less punishment than boys. But they are also made more anxious about the withdrawal of love.[72]

Thus, specific methods of child training and the cultural definition of femininity (which necessitates reliance on the approval of others) both encourage dependency in women. Kagan links the crucial significance of others—and their acceptance or rejection—to the finding that girls are often more conforming and more concerned about socially desirable behavior than boys.[73] Another interpretation of female conformity links it to doll-play training. David Matza has hypothesized that girls are taught to be more conforming and concerned with socially acceptable behavior because they are trained to act as socializing agents with their dolls. By talking to, and "training" their dolls to do the right thing, the girls themselves gain a vast amount of experience in articulating and sanctioning the cultural norms.[74]

SOME EMPIRICAL OBSERVATIONS

Until recently most psychologists who have written about the process of sex role learning either have relied solely on their own observations, or have applied more general theories of learning to the specific case of sex roles. Thus a major gap in the literature has been the absence of observational evidence to support (or refute or modify) the theories discussed above. However, in the past few years Professor Lisa A. Serbin and her colleagues have conducted a series of pioneering observational studies that have begun to yield some evidence to support these theories.

In one study Serbin *et al.* observed fifteen preschool classrooms to examine teacher responses to boys and girls working and playing in the same setting.[75] More specifically, they coded how the teachers responded to two types of behavior—disruption and dependency—to see if they differentially reinforced these behaviors in boys and girls.

Contrary to what one might assume, earlier research had indicated that teacher attention to disruptive behavior served to *encourage* it rather than to discourage it. For example, O'Leary, Kaufman, Kass, and Drabman found that "teachers' loud reprimands reinforced and maintained disruptive behavior at a high level, while soft reprimands, audible only to the child and his neighbors, effectively decreased disruption."[76] In other studies, "rates of aggressive behavior in preschool children were shown experimentally to decrease when the behavior was ignored by the teacher."[77] Thus Serbin *et al.* reasoned that if teachers were more likely to respond to aggression or disruptive behavior in boys, and to do so with loud reprimands, they might be reinforcing such behavior, and "one might expect boys to become and/or remain more disruptive than the girls."[78]

In accord with their hypotheses, Serbin *et al.* found that the preschool teachers were indeed more likely to respond to disruptive behavior from boys.[79] This difference was clearest with respect to aggression: "The average rate of teacher response to aggression was over three times higher for boys than for girls."[80] The researchers also found that teachers used more loud reprimands when scolding boys.

In response to dependent behaviors, girls got more attention when they stood or played near the teacher. In fact, the researchers found that the girls received a lot of attention from the teacher *only* when they were near the teacher, not when they moved farther away. This suggests that girls stayed close to the teacher to avoid being ignored. There were no similar proximity contingencies for boys: "Boys received a fairly constant rate of teacher attention regardless of their distance from the teacher."[81]

After the observations were completed, the researchers asked the teachers to respond to a questionnaire. The teachers' responses indicated that they "were not aware of responding differentially to boys and girls, or of giving different amounts of positive or instructional attention to either sex."[82]

In trying to interpret their findings Serbin *et al.* asked why the "teachers respond more frequently and intensively to the aggressive behavior of boys. One possibility is that disruption by boys is . . . more intense or dangerous than the disruptive behavior of girls, and

. . . teachers feel a greater necessity to react . . . forcefully. Another possibility is that teachers believe boys to be less responsive to reprimand . . . , and habitually give them more 'intensive' attention."[83] The authors concluded that while either or both possibilities "may represent real sex differences in behavior, the resulting patterns of teacher attention are those which should differentially maintain, or even strengthen, existing levels of disruptive behavior in boys."[84]

It is interesting to note the parallel findings between this research and Serbin's television study. In both settings females are more likely to be ignored, and Serbin hypothesizes that, as a result, they learn to feel ineffectual and unable to influence the world.

THE RESULTS: SEX DIFFERENCES IN BEHAVIOR

While we will be reviewing sex differences in behavior throughout this book, it may be useful to discuss briefly the best-documented sex difference: as psychologist Carol Jacklin notes, "the clearest sex difference in social behavior is in aggression."[85] Boys at all ages are more aggressive* than girls, and men are more aggressive than women.

For example, in one study defining aggression among children as pushing or hitting without smiling, Omark, Omark, and Edelman collected extensive time-sampled observations of children in playgrounds in the United States, Switzerland, and Ethiopia. In all three countries the boys were consistently more aggressive than the girls.[86] Similarly, in experiments with children four and five years of age, Parton and Geshuri noted that boys were more likely than girls to imitate videotaped aggressive responses toward dolls and other toys.[87] In a third study, which observed eight- and nine-year-old children, Slaby found that boys were more likely than girls to deliver "punches" to an unseen peer by pressing a button.[88] And in observations of eleven-year-old children, Shortell and Biller found boys more likely than girls to deliver a higher intensity of noise to an unseen peer."[89]

The manifestation of aggression depends somewhat on the age of the subjects. "In nursery age children, aggression is usually very

*Jacklin defines aggression as the intent to hurt another. Assertion, on the other hand, implies standing up for one's own rights, but without intending to hurt.

21

direct and physical, and thus easily measured . . . [A]s children get older, verbal aggression becomes more common, and physical aggression becomes less common."[90] But either way, according to Jacklin, whether verbally or physically, boys are more aggressive than girls.[91]

Similar sex differences are found in dominance behavior, which is closely linked to aggression. As Jacklin notes, "toughness" hierarchies tend to develop in the early grades so that boys and girls can reliably tell you which kids are "tougher" than which others, and these hierarchies are mostly composed of boys.[92] She hypothesizes that these hierarchies may grow out of the different sized play groups that boys and girls tend to form, for boys are more likely to play in larger groups. In nursery school, for example, among children without prior school experience, boys tend to play in groups of five, on the average, while girls tend to play in groups of two or three. Dominance hierarchies are more likely to develop in larger groups than in dyads or triads.[93]

Some evidence also suggests two types of cognitive sex differences: verbal abilities and spatial abilities. These abilities are discussed in Chapter 3.

Variation in

sex role standards

and behavior

Chapter 2

INDIVIDUAL DIFFERENCES

Thus far we have taken the success of the socialization process for granted and have assumed that most boys and girls eventually adopt the prescribed sex role behaviors. But most of us can think of exceptions—the self-confident achievement-oriented girl, or the dependent boy who cares very much about others' opinions of him. We all know some people who seem to contradict the stereotypes and others, possibly including ourselves, who conform only to a percentage of them. In fact, we may often feel the pull of the extremes of a single trait within ourselves, wanting to be both independent and dependent at the same time, or feeling that we are at times totally oriented toward achievement and at other times holding back for fear of being too successful.

In an effort to summarize a large body of literature, I have focused on the "average" girl (and boy) and have attempted to describe the "typical" pattern of socialization. As a result, the wide range of variation in individual behavior has been obscured. It is important to pause in this analysis to emphasize the extent of variation among individuals of *both* sexes with regard to personality characteristics, intelligence, and achievement motivation.

The range of differences within each sex is much greater than the differences between the average members of opposite sexes.[1] Whenever we speak of averages, we obscure the great range of variation within each sex. Moreover, after a review of the literature on sex differences, Jo Freeman concluded that what was deemed typical of one sex or the other was based on the average performance of only *two-thirds* of the subjects.[2] But this disregards the behavior of the *remaining one-third* of each sex. Because it is easier to describe the "typical" socialization pattern first, however, we will continue temporarily to "disregard" individual differences. In the final chapter of this book, we will return to the topic of individual behavior variation and examine its implications for socialization theory.

As we describe the "typical" socialization process, however, the reader should keep in mind the limits of all generalizations. While most descriptions may accurately characterize most boys and girls, there will always be an important minority who "deviate" from the typical pattern. In addition, those who are in the majority and those who are in the minority are always shifting—so that an individual may be "typical" at one point, or in one type of behavior, but "deviant" at other times.

THE CONTINUING RESEARCH DEBATE

Before we continue, it is important to note that there is still considerable disagreement about the extent to which sex-linked behavioral differences actually exist. Although the earlier research seemed to confirm the existence of differences,[3] many of these findings are now considered open to question. For example, in 1974 psychologists Maccoby and Jacklin undertook a massive re-evaluation and updating of the empirical evidence on sex differences.[4] They reviewed approximately 1,600 studies, published primarily between 1966 and 1973, and concluded that many of the earlier reports of sex differences were unfounded.

Maccoby and Jacklin report that the evidence is equivocal with respect to anxiety, level of activity, competitiveness, dominance, compliance, and nurturance. In addition, although they find fairly solid support for the long-established behavioral differences in verbal ability, spatial ability, and aggressiveness, they do *not* find substantial support for previously reported findings that: (1) girls are more "social" than boys, (2) girls are more "suggestible" than boys, (3) girls have lower self-esteem, or (4) girls are less motivated toward achievement.[5]

Given the political and emotional investments in the debate over sex differences in behavior, it is unlikely that any work on this topic will be accepted as definitive in the near future. Thus it is not surprising that while most scholars have praised the Maccoby-Jacklin effort as the most authoritative analysis in the field, others contend it is biased in the direction of finding no sex differences. For example, as we have noted, they necessarily relied on studies of very young children, which may have led to an underestimation of sex differences that appear only in the late years, particularly in adolescence.[6] However, inasmuch as they reviewed all the published research of their colleagues in psychology, one cannot blame Maccoby and Jacklin for this bias. It originates in the field itself.

SOCIAL CLASS VARIATION IN SEX ROLES

Sex role standards also differ by social class and by racial and ethnic group.[7] And even within these large subgroupings, various aspects of family composition affect both the content and the potency of sex role socialization. Because it is impossible to consider all these factors in each section of this book, we have focused on the most prevalent section of the population, the broadly defined white middle class. This may have given the reader an erroneous impression of uniformity. Thus, it is important now to consider some of the

LIBRARY
OF
MOUNT ST. MARY'S
COLLEGE

variations in sex role standards by social class. In the next section we will consider variation by race.

A parent's social class position is an important determinant of his or her sex role standards and expectations. Sociologists have generally used a combination of three indicators to measure social class—education, occupation, and income. However, the research on sex role socialization has been consistent no matter what indicator of class is used. All the studies have found that persons in the higher social classes tend to be less rigid about sex distinctions. In working-class and lower-class families, there is much more concern about different roles for boys and girls and men and women. As Letha and John Scanzoni have pointed out, the theme song of the popular television program *All In The Family* accurately portrays the concern of a working-class father (Archie Bunker) for clear-cut distinctions between the sexes (for the days "when girls were girls and men were men").[8]

As might be expected from these parental expectations, differentiation between boys and girls appears to be sharpest in lower-class families.[9] Rabban found that children from working-class families differentiate sex roles at earlier ages and have more traditional sex role standards than middle-class children.[10] He showed that working-class boys were aware of the appropriate sex-typed toy choices by age four or five; middle-class boys were not aware of them until age six.[11] The class differences are even greater for girls. Middle-class girls not only showed later awareness of sex-typing than working-class girls, but were less traditional in their sex role concepts.[12]

Middle-class parents may encourage "traditional feminine behavior" in their daughters, but they also encourage a degree of independence and assertiveness. Not only are middle-class parents willing to "tolerate" daughters who are tomboys, many of them encourage their daughters to do well in sports and to excel in school. Lower-class parents are more likely to view such interests and achievements as "too masculine" and to discourage them.

A similar pattern emerges in the class-related sex role expectations for boys. Middle-class parents are willing to let their sons be more expressive (to be more nurturant and tender), while working-class parents see these traits as "too feminine" or sissy.[13] Working-class parents want their sons to be instrumental, that is, to be focused on tasks and work.

In summary, then, middle-class parents are interested in seeing both their sons and their daughters develop a greater range of traits along *both* instrumental and expressive lines. In contrast, blue-collar parents encourage traditional sex role behavior in both boys and girls. These differences are illustrated by Lillian Rubin's comparative interviews with lower- and middle-class families. As Rubin notes, in the homes of the professional middle class, both boys and girls

> have more training in exploring the socio-emotional realm. . . . It's true that for the girls, this usually is the *focus* of their lives, while for the boys, it is not. Nevertheless, compared to child-rearing patterns in working-class families, professional middle-class families make fewer and less rigid sex role distinctions in early childhood. . . .
>
> As small children, therefore, boys in such middle-class homes more often get the message that it's all right to cry, to be nurturant as well as nurtured, to be reflective and intro-spective, even at times to be passive—in essence, in some small measure, to relate to their expressive side.
>
> Not once in a professional middle-class homes did I see a young boy shake his father's hand in a well-taught "manly" gesture as he bid him good night. Not once did I hear a middle-class parent scornfully—or even sympathetically—call a crying boy a sissy or in any way reprimand him for his tears. Yet, these were not uncommon observations in the working-class homes I visited. Indeed, I was impressed with the fact that, even as young as six or seven, the working-class boys seemed more emotionally controlled—more like miniature men—than those in the middle-class families.[14]

In later chapters we will trace the ways in which these class differences affect scholastic achievements and the choice of marriage and/or career.

ETHNIC VARIATION IN SEX ROLES

Further specification of sex role standards occurs along ethnic and racial lines. Many people have the impression that Italians, Jews,

Asian Americans, Chicanos, Irish, Poles, Blacks, and Puerto Ricans have distinctive conceptions of appropriate behavior for men and women.[15] With few exceptions, however, ethnic variation in sex role standards has been ignored in the socialization literature.[16]

One fascinating study, conducted by Fred Strodbeck, compared the socialization practices of Italian and Jewish mothers in encouraging achievement motivation in their sons.[17] When asked about their aspirations for their sons' achievements, both Italian and Jewish mothers had equally high standards and hopes for their performance. However, when asked how they would respond to their sons' hypothetical failure to meet their high standards, the Italian mothers indicated they would nevertheless love and accept the sons. The Jewish mothers, in contrast, reported they would show displeasure if their sons failed to meet their standards, and moreover they would make their love and acceptance contingent upon the sons' continued striving and eventual success. Strodbeck concluded that the Jewish mothers' "contingent love" was far more powerful in creating high achievement motivation in boys.

Unfortunately, most of the research on achievement motivation and ethnic differences in socialization, like Strodbeck's, focuses exclusively on male samples. As psychologist Matina Horner has noted, most social scientists investigating achievement motivation did not consider women's achievement important enough to investigate.[18] Further, those few who originally included women in their samples later dropped the female respondents from their analysis when they found the females' responses did not conform to the male pattern.

RACIAL VARIATION IN SEX ROLES: THE CASE OF BLACK WOMEN

When one first approaches the question of sex roles among black women one cannot help but be puzzled by two seemingly contradictory findings. Some researchers report that black women have adopted a more masculine sex role than white women and are strong, assertive, and independent. But other studies have shown that their self-images are even more sex-stereotyped than those of white women.

In this section we will briefly review the research in support of each of these views, and then try to make some sense of the apparent contradictions.[19] However, it is important to note that sex role research on blacks still remains one of the biggest "blind spots in existing sociology.[20] Clearly, more systematic research in this area is sorely needed.

The sociologists who assert that black women are strong, independent, and dominant trace these attributes to their role in the family and the economy. They point to the legacy of slavery for the roots of the black family structure, and to black woman's historically greater access to occupational opportunities, money, and status.

The black family has frequently been characterized as a matriarchal (mother-headed) extended family with an emphasis on consanguine relationships (i.e., blood ties) rather than on conjugal (husband-wife) relationships.[21] Although sociologists, such as Kandel[22] and Moynihan,[23] have found that there are more female-headed families among blacks even when the socioeconomic status is controlled, the matriarchal family structure is typically a lower-class family pattern.

This lower-class pattern begins, according to Stack, with premarital pregnancy.[24] Since premarital sex is prevalent and parenthood is highly valued (regardless of the child's legitimacy), young women often become pregnant in their teens.[25] However, youth and lack of monetary resources often prevent them from marrying and establishing a separate domicile, so many are unmarried and living in their parents' homes when their first child is born. Thereafter, these unmarried women quickly and accurately assess the relative stability of welfare, as opposed to the extreme economic vulnerability of their male partners, and commonly forgo legal marriage, at least temporarily.[26]

Since these unmarried mothers often stay at home, it is likely that their mothers will play a great role in raising the grandchild. Even married adult children often continue to reside with one or more of their parents, and if a marriage fails, both men and women readily return to their mother's household. Thus the "matriarch" is both the head of the household and the dominant authority figure in many black families. She also provides a strong female role model.

Stack attributes the lack of permanent husband-wife households to two primary factors. The first is the lack of permanent well-paying jobs for men.[27] The second is the disincentives built into the welfare system.[28] As a result, many researchers, report that black women, in contrast to white women, "hold more negative attitudes toward the reliability of men and the security and desirability of marriage."[29] They realize that they cannot rely on men for their support and they socialize their daughters to have the same realistic skepticism. For example, Ladner found that very young black girls originally want to marry a man who is a protector, supporter, and companion. However, with increasing age they come to believe that very few men can fulfill these roles, and they become more ambivalent in their expectations. (Some girls had firmly established the view that men are "no good" by the time they were eight years old.)[30]

Having learned that they cannot count on men or marriage for their future security, black girls realize that they will have to rely on themselves. As a student of mine wrote in an autobiographical socialization paper, "Black girls don't dream of being rescued by 'Prince Charming.' They know that 'Snow White' is White, and that if they want to get something or somewhere, they are going to have to get it themselves."[31] Thus black girls are socialized to become self-sufficient and to rely on their own achievements.

As Ladner notes, the realities of life in the ghetto, where aggressiveness and toughness are requisites for survival, make the ideal of a dependent, passive, middle-class housewife almost unimaginable.[32] The black girl is given responsibility for herself (and sometimes for the home and her younger siblings as well) from an early age and is expected to learn to "fend for herself."

At the same time that the black girl is learning the importance of becoming self-sufficient, her observations of her mother's work role (and her mother's attitude toward work) provide a practical guide toward this end. Because a significant proportion of black women have always worked in the paid labor force, both they and their daughters are more likely to regard work as a normal part of the female role.[33] In fact, employed black women are more likely to hold professional positions than are employed black men, and Epstein has shown that the "double negative" status of being both a woman and a black may actually help a black woman to gain access to the professions that both white women and black men have found difficult to penetrate.[34]

Thus, in contrast to the traditional sex-stereotyped view of work and careers as "masculine" pursuits, in the black community they are seen as natural and acceptable female roles. Work brings money, security, and status—all of which are highly valued by both men and women.

Because black women are more likely to regard work as part of the "normal" female role, they are more likely to encourage and support their daughters' educational and occupational aspirations. Thus, Kandel found that black mothers in female-headed families had higher educational aspirations for their daughters than for their sons.[35]

There are also data to suggest that the daughters absorb their mothers' aspirations. Ladner found that young black girls most frequently identify with and aspire to be a "strong black woman"— resourceful, hardworking, and economically independent.[36] The teenage girls she interviewed saw this ideal woman as the one who kept the home intact—by caring for children, carrying out household tasks, and often supporting the family financially. Another popular aspiration was to acquire the skills that would allow the girl to escape from the ghetto and become an educated and upwardly mobile middle-class woman.[37]

Thus, to summarize the first position, there is considerable evidence to support the assertion that young black girls are socialized to become independent, self-reliant, and self-sufficient "strong women." In fact, Ladner has shown that black girls are encouraged to be more independent than white girls, irrespective of social class.[38]

Other research, however, suggests that black women are socialized to accept a traditional female role. For example, Gurin and Gaylord, writing in 1976, found that sex role influences inhibit the career and educational aspirations of black women in approximately the same ways as white women, and that black and white college women alike continue to be interested in the same traditionally "feminine fields."[39] For example, women of both races are more likely to aspire to be a high school teacher rather than a lawyer.

Similarly, for both races, fewer women than men are interested in business or engineering. They conclude that their "results agree with those of earlier studies which indicate that women students of both races tend to have lower aspirations than their male counterparts."[40]

Hershey also reports that black college women ascribe to the same sex-stereotyped identities as white college women.[41] She found that the primary difference in sex role attitudes among college students is between men and women, not between blacks and whites. Both black and white college women described themselves as tender, gentle, sensitive, and compassionate.* Similarly, both black and white college males described themselves as assertive, having leadership abilities, and having a strong personality. In fact, she found that black men scored higher on masculinity than white men, indicating their "affinity for more traditional patriarchal sex role norms."[42] Thus Hershey concluded that since both black women and black men ascribe to traditional sex role attitudes, sex is much more important than race in determining sex role identities.

How can we reconcile these seemingly contradictory findings?

One explanation lies in the social class differences in the research samples. It is possible that lower-class black girls are socialized to be strong and independent but middle-class blacks are not. We know that the mother-headed family, a major source of the strong, self-reliant female role, is much more common among the lower classes. This may explain why Stack and Ladner, who studied lower-class girls, found them to be self-sufficient and strong. However, Hershey, Gurin and Gaylord, who focused on (mostly middle-class) black college women, found more traditional aspirations and attitudes.**

A second explanation lies in the difference between idealized roles and actual behavior. It is possible that Hershey, Gurin and

---

*In addition, she found that black women were significantly more stereotyped than white women in their sex role *attitudes,* although they scored higher than white women on the masculine dimension of the sex role *identity* scale.

**If black women from lower-class families are being socialized into less traditional sex roles than those from middle-class families, then social class has an opposite effect in black and white families: while white lower-class families are more sex-stereotyped than white middle-class families, black lower-class families may be *less* sex stereotyped than black middle-class families.

Gaylord, using questionnaires (which often elicit socially desirable responses), elicited female "ideals," while Stack and Ladner, who conducted lengthy interviews with their respondents "in the field," captured more of their actual behavior. As Hershey herself notes, attitudes and self ratings may not be congruent with behavior.[43] In fact, she suggests that women who take on traditionally masculine tasks may still identify with the ideal-typical female role, and that some would prefer a more sex-stereotyped life if they had the option.[44]

A third way of resolving these findings is to recognize that they are not contradictory at all—each may reflect a different aspect of the black woman's multi-dimensional sex role. Thus black women may be more independent, more self-reliant, and more work-oriented than white women, but, at the same time, they may be as sensitive, nurturant, compassionate, and "feminine." The findings are contradictory only if we assume that "masculinity" and "femininity" are unidimensional.

Women, and black women in particular, may have some "masculine traits" such as independence and self-sufficiency, *and* some traditional "feminine" characteristics, such as warmth and nurturance. For example, in his study of sex roles in the black community John Scanzoni found that he had to consider several different role dimensions—each of which varied independently. He found that blacks were more "traditional" with respect to approved behavior for men and women, but were less traditional with respect to women's individualism.[45] In addition, black women were both more nurturant and more task competent, and had more autonomy and power in the family. Thus these findings, like those reviewed above, indicate that "masculine" and "feminine" attributes cannot be viewed as polar opposites.

Similarly, Bem has shown that individuals can score high on both masculinity and femininity, low on both, or some combination of the two.[46] Further, a lot of sex role behavior is likely to be *situationally specific*—that is, it is likely to depend on the social context. For example, a woman attorney may be assertive with clients, aggressive in court, tender with her husband, and nurturant with her children. In fact, since sex role attitudes and behaviors are

likely to be much more *situationally specific* than the research literature seems to acknowledge, it is surprising that there have not been
more seemingly contradictory findings—for both blacks and whites.

FAMILY CONSTELLATION AND SEX ROLES

In addition to class and race, another important variable in sex
role behavior is the family constellation—the number, spacing, and
sex ratio of the children in the family. Brim has pointed out the
importance of siblings in sex role definitions, finding that children
with cross-sex siblings exhibited more traits of the opposite sex than
did those with same-sex siblings.[47] This effect was particularly strong
when opposite-sex siblings were older. Thus, boys with older sisters
and girls with older brothers are more likely to exhibit the traits of
the opposite sex.

Another significant aspect of family constellation is the number
and presence of adults. Many sociologists have assumed that children
who grow up without a father or a mother must be inadequately
socialized. However, recent research has indicated that father absence
does not affect lower-class boys' occupational achievement, although
it may have a depressant effect for middle- and upper-class boys.

On the other hand, the single-parent mother-headed family
may be a spur to occupational achievement in girls. Hunt and Hunt
have found that girls in father-absent families are freed from the
ideal-typical female socialization.[48] These families establish a new
type of female role model, blurring the traditional distinction between
male and female roles and the instrumental/expressive division of
labor by sex, because mothers are performing both roles and both
types of tasks. Thus, father absence, in conjunction with modifica-
tions of the mother role, may remove some of the conventional
barriers to female occupational aspirations and achievement. When
girls are not socialized into sharply differentiated sex roles, they
may be freed from the traditional restraints on female achievement.

The school

years

Chapter 3

Although boys and girls learn sex roles early, the definition of appropriate sex role behavior changes with age. The female sex role at age five is specific to the attributes of a five-year-old, and different from the female sex role at age twenty-five.[1] Sex role socialization continues throughout the child's life as she or he learns age-specific sex role behavior.

Thus far we have focused largely on socialization within the family. As the child matures and begins to participate in social relations outside the family, teachers, peers, and other socializing agents become more significant in defining and sanctioning appropriate sex role behavior.

THE INFLUENCE OF THE SCHOOL

Once the child enters school, her or his experiences there assume great importance. The educational system has generally reinforced sex role stereotypes. One of the first messages communicated to girls at school is that they are less important than boys. For example, in a 1960 study of all third grade readers published since 1930, Child, Potter, and Levine found 73 percent of the stories were about male characters.[2] Girls' impressions that they are not very important are reinforced by the portrait of the few women who do appear in the texts. Child *et al.* found girls and women shown as timid, inactive, unambitious, and uncreative. Females were not only the moral inferiors of males in these books (they are shown to be lazy twice as often as males), but their intellectual inferiors as well:

> The persons who supply information are predominantly male. ... Males, in short, are being portrayed as the bearers of knowledge and wisdom, and as the persons through whom knowledge can come to the child.[3]

More recent examinations of elementary school readers indicate that even the newest textbooks retain the same stereotypes.[4] Nor are these stereotypes restricted to readers. Weitzman and Rizzo have found that spelling, mathematics, science, and social studies textbooks purvey an equally limited image of women.[5] Rarely are women mentioned in important roles in history, as government leaders, or as great scientists. This study found the stereotyping to be most extreme in the science textbooks, where only 6 percent of the pictures included adult women. Weitzman and Rizzo hypothesize that the presentation of science as a prototypical masculine endeavor may help to explain how young girls are "cooled out" of science and channeled into more traditional "feminine" fields.[6]

Educational achievement tests reflect a similar masculine bias. In a study of the achievement tests from each of the major publishing companies, psychologist Carol Kehr Tittle found "a substantial bias" in both the number of male and female noun and pronoun references, and in the stereotyped portrayals of males and females in the content of the test items.[7] The test items much more frequently referred to males and the male world. In addition, a content analysis of each of the tests revealed sex role stereotypes in the questions:

> Women were portrayed almost exclusively as homemakers or in
> the pursuit of hobbies ("Mrs. Jones, the President of the Garden
> Club . . .") [and] young girls carry out "female chores" (Father
> helps Betty and Tom build a playhouse; when it's completed,
> "Betty sets out dishes on the table, while Tom carries in the
> chairs . . ."). . . .
>
> In numerous activity-centered items, boys were shown
> playing, climbing, camping, hiking, taking on roles of responsi-
> bility and leadership. Girls help with the cooking, buy ribbon
> and vegetables, and, when participating in any active pursuit,
> take the back seat to the stronger, more qualified boys (Buddy
> says to Clara, "Oh, I guess it's all right for us boys to help girls.
> I've done some good turns for girls myself, because I'm a
> Scout.").[8]

The adult roles in the test items were equally stereotyped.
Most of the biographies were about men. All the professors, doctors,
and presidents of companies were listed as male, while practically all
teachers were listed as female. If a team was mentioned, it usually
had all male members. In addition, as Tittle observes, some questions
implied that the majority of professions are closed to women. For
example, "a reading comprehension passage about the characteristics
and qualifications required for the Presidency began with the statement: 'In the United States, voters do not directly choose the man
they wish to be President.' It repeatedly says 'he must be,' 'he must
have. . . .'"[9]

Most schools have had a sex-stereotyped tracking system in
which girls are channeled into the more "feminine" subjects (English
and social studies in academic high schools, typing and bookkeeping
in commercial high schools) while boys are encouraged to tackle the
"hard sciences." For example, in the 1970 courses listed in *The
Public High Schools of New York City,* seventy-seven are designated
"technical courses restricted to males," and thirty-six are designated
for females.

Tracking systems have not only channeled the two sexes into
two different vocational directions, but have further served to keep
both boys and girls from learning skills useful in later life. Thus girls

37

who have been excluded from shop have not learned how to fix things around the home, and boys excluded from home economics are kept blissfully ignorant of cooking and other domestic skills.

The magnitude of the skewed sorting of students into "sex-appropriate" vocational tracks is reflected in 1972 nationwide data reported by Saario, Jacklin, and Tittle:

> Ninety-five percent of all students registered in vocational agriculture courses are male; 93 percent of all students registered in consumer and homemaking courses are female; 85 percent of those enrolled in home economics courses which lead to gainful employment are female; 92 percent of those registered in technical courses—metallurgy, engineering, oceanography, police science—are male; 75 percent in office occupations are female; and 89 percent of all registered in trade and industrial courses are male.[10]

In the past, girls have also been excluded from most rigorous sports and from school athletic teams. "In fact, the disparity in support for boys' and girls' athletic programs is perhaps the single most visible piece of discrimination in American education. In 1971, boys' participation in high school sports was 12 times that of girls."[11]

Hopefully, all this is beginning to change with the passage of Title IX (of the Education Amendments of 1972), which forbids all forms of sex-based discrimination in educational institutions. However, a comprehensive report on HEW's progress in enforcing Title IX concludes that as of 1978 "rules and policies that perpetuate unequal treatment of males and females—which are now clearly illegal—are still going on uncorrected in the nation's schools."[12] Some cases cited in this report indicate how far we still have to go:

> A ninth grader in Livonia, Michigan, wanted to learn how to handle power tools, but shop classes were off limits for girls. "Women," she was told, "should stick to home ec." She wrote the government for help in 1973. Three years later, HEW wrote back, got no answer, and closed the case. The government never checked to find out if girls were still barred from taking shop.

> "Something is wrong! I am doing more work for less pay," a New Jersey woman wrote HEW in September 1973. She was

coaching four girls' teams for one-third of what the school paid men to coach the team. HEW left her complaint in limbo for three years before closing it without an investigation.

One high school senior recounted the way a counselor in Los Angeles tried to discourage her from pursuing a career as a veterinarian. "She said," the girl wrote, "that at our age it's the maternal instinct, and after a few years of college we outgrow it." The worst thing about all these messages is that girls believe them.[13]

THE INFLUENCE OF TEACHERS

Guidance counselors and teachers can either help to reinforce conformity to the traditional female role, or present exciting new role models to impressionable young girls. In the past they have mostly done the former.

Until recently we have known very little about what actually goes on in the classroom. However, in recent years a number of observational studies have been undertaken to examine the role of the teacher in creating or reinforcing sex role stereotypes. In Chapter 1 we discussed Serbin's studies of preschool classes and her finding that girls' proximal behavior (i.e., staying close to the teacher) and boys' disruptive behavior are reinforced by teacher attention.[14]

In a similar observational study of teachers' behavior in elementary school classes (among sixth grade children), Meyer and Thompson found that boys receive much more disapproval and behavioral criticism from their teachers.[15] These teacher responses, according to Serbin's theory, selectively reinforce disruptive behavior in boys.

In another set of pioneering observational studies Professor Carol Dweck and her colleagues Bush, Davidson, Nelson, and Enna set out to examine how girls acquire "learned helplessness."[16] Learned helplessness exists when children reduce their effort because they assume that failure is insurmountable. Children perceive failure as insurmountable when they attribute it to stable, uncontrollable factors, such as lack of ability.[17] Children who exhibit learned helplessness typically react to a failure by giving up or by deteriorated

39

performance. In contrast, children who believe they can overcome failure tend to view it as a result of unstable, controllable factors, such as effort. After a failure experience, these children often show heightened persistence and improved performance.

Girls are more likely than boys to exhibit learned helplessness. They are likely to blame a poor performance on their own lack of ability, while boys are likely to emphasize motivational factors (and to say they did not try hard enough).[18] Even when girls are proficient at a task, they are more likely to assume that a failure reflects lack of ability and subsequently to do less well at the task. Boys at the same level of ability are more likely to assume that the failure was "a mistake," to try harder, and subsequently to improve their performance.

In order to understand why boys ignore the feedback of a failure experience, Dweck *et al.* hypothesized that "frequent and widespread use of negative evaluation for boys negates the failure feedback they receive from adults as valid indicators of their ability."[19] Because they receive so much negative feedback, boys come to view it as either irrelevant to their performance or a result of their lack of motivation.[20] In contrast, these researchers hypothesized that "the more sparing and discriminating use of negatives for girls makes negative evaluation particularly informative about their level of ability."[21] They further hypothesized that "frequent use of feedback for nonintellectual behavior (conduct and nonintellectual aspects of work like neatness) should increase the ambiguity of that feedback and impair its meaning as an evaluation of the intellectual quality of the child's work."[22]

These hypotheses were generally supported. In their own words their findings were as follows:

> First, on positive feedback, more than 90 percent of all the positive feedback that boys received was addressed specifically to the intellectual quality of their performance; for girls, less than 80 percent referred to the intellectual quality of their work.
>
> Second, on negative feedback, the discrepancy was more marked. Less than one third of the boys' negative evaluation was contingent on intellectual aspects of their work, whereas

more than two thirds of girls' was directly related to the quality of their performance.

Third, when only the work-related feedback was examined, differences in evaluative feedback for the two sexes were again apparent. . . . For boys, over 90 percent of the praise they received for their work was praise for intellectual competence; whereas for girls, significantly less of their praise (80.9 percent) was directed at the intellectual aspects [of their work]. In other words, almost 20 percent of positive evaluation girls received for their work referred to intellectually irrelevant aspects, such as neatness.

Fourth, for negative work-related evaluations, the sex differences were more pronounced. For boys, only 54.4 percent of the work-related criticism referred to intellectual inadequacy; the remaining criticism was for failure to obey the rules of form. In contrast, 88.9 percent of work-related criticism to girls was specifically addressed to intellectual performance; little criticism pertained to violations of rules of form.[23]

Clearly, the fourth finding is extremely important, for if 45 percent of the negative evaluation boys received for their work indicated only that they did not follow the rules of form, it is easy to see how boys can view negative feedback as irrelevant to the intellectual quality of their performance. The authors conclude that their studies "demonstrate that the pattern of evaluative feedback given to boys and girls in the classroom can result directly in girls' greater tendency to view failure feedback as indicative of their level of ability."[24]

INTELLECTUAL AND ANALYTIC ABILITY

Girls consistently do better than boys in reading, mathematics, and speaking until they reach high school, but at that point their performance in school and on ability tests begins to drop.[25] Although we have every reason to believe that girls' intellectual achievements do decline during high school, it should be noted that the typical measures of intelligence and scholastic achievement at this age have a strong male bias. Milton found that when adolescent or adult subjects were presented with problems involving primarily mathematical or geometric reasoning, the males consistently obtained higher scores than females.[26] However, if the problem—involving identical logical steps and computations—dealt with "feminine content" such as cooking and gardening materials, the women scored much better than if the problem dealt with guns, money, or geometric designs.[27] Apparently the typical female believes that the ability to solve problems involving geometry, physics, or logic is a uniquely masculine skill, and her motivation even to attack such problems is low—for unusual excellence in solving them may be equated with loss of femininity.[28]

Since the erroneous finding that women are less analytic than men is often quoted, it deserves some attention here. It has been postulated that analytic thinking is developed by early independence training: how soon a child is encouraged to assume initiative, to take responsibility for herself or himself, and to solve problems alone rather than to rely on others for help or direction.[29] Each of these characteristics, as already reviewed, is encouraged in boys and discouraged in girls. When women are socialized to be dependent and passive, they are supposedly being trained to be more "field-dependent" or "contextual" and less analytic in their thinking.

In a devastating review of the scientific literature on what is usually called analytic ability, Sherman has pointed out that the term analytic ability is misleading.[30] It implies a general intellectual skill, whereas what is apparently being measured in most of the studies is the much more limited ability of spatial perception—the ability to visualize objects out of their context.[31] Boys are generally "field independent" in their spatial perception, whereas girls are more "contextual." Girls score lower on tests of spatial relationships, but in verbal perception—certainly an area that is equally, if not more, important in analytic thinking—they score higher than boys.[32]

It seems ironic that researchers have labeled spatial perception "analytic ability." One might speculate that if women had higher scores on spatial perception and men had higher scores on verbal perception, the latter would have been called analytic ability—for what the researchers have done is to seize upon one of the few traits in which males score higher and label it analytic ability.

Actually, spatial ability has little to do with analytic thinking in any of the usual meanings of that term.[33] Strictly analytic ability has to do with the structure of arguments, the logical closure of propositions and syllogisms, and patterns of logic. Since World War I (in the work of Whitehead and Russell), and certainly by the 1930's with Wittgenstein's work in modern logic, we generally understand that the underlying structure of logic (and thus of mathematics as well) is ultimately a language pattern, resting on our understanding of linguistic connections. One might therefore argue that people who excel at language and show the most facility in language analysis and construction would potentially have the greatest ability in analytic thinking—in the perception of logical connections and in the understanding of the strength or weakness of arguments.[34] However, this would lead us to conclude that women have superior analytic ability, and the strong anti-female bias pervading the literature on intelligence and analytic thinking precludes this logical conclusion.

It is interesting to note that spatial ability appears to be learned, and is especially strong in individuals who have hobbies or jobs of a mechanical or technical nature. Since the sex disparity in skills related to this ability widens greatly at age seventeen, it is tempting to connect the superior performance of males with the training they receive in high school classes in mechanical drawing, analytic geometry, and shop (as well as with their spare-time activities).

In fact, Fennema and Sherman found that once they controlled for the number of space-related courses a student had taken, the sex difference in spatial visualization disappeared.[35] They conclude that such sex differences as do exist in spatial ability are most likely explained by factors such as sex-segregated tracking systems and the encouragement of mathematical and mechanical skills in boys.[36] Thus, if both spatial and verbal ability can be learned, findings of sex differences in these areas should direct us once again to the socialization process.

THE INFLUENCE OF PARENTS

It is not the school alone that channels girls and boys in different directions and emphasizes certain skills over others. Parents also have different sex-related expectations. Aberle and Naegele have reported that middle-class fathers show concern over their sons' lack of aggressiveness, good school performance, responsibility, and initiative. In contrast, their concerns for their daughters focus on attractiveness and popularity. As the authors report:

> In all of these categories boys were the object of concern . . . ; satisfaction with girls seemed to focus strongly on their daughters being nice, sweet, pretty, affectionate, and well liked.[37]

With respect to future careers for their daughters, half of the fathers rejected the possibility out of hand. The other half said they would accept the possibility, but preferred and expected their daughters to marry—a career was unnecessary. Only two of the twenty fathers said they wanted their daughters to know how to earn a living.[38]

The Aberle and Naegele study was done in 1952 and is now rather dated. However, more recent studies of parental influence on their children's educational aspirations indicate that girls are still less likely to receive parental support than boys. Sewell and Shah found that parents continue to encourage their sons more than their daughters.[39] Similarly, most of Bordua's male adolescents reported that their parents "stress college a lot," whereas most of the girls reported that their parents "don't care one way or the other."[40] Elder suggested that parents put a differential stress on college for boys, and that the financial support that has typically accompanied their concern may have had more of an effect in determining the college plans of adolescents than their own intentions.[41]

Parental pressures to follow a traditional female role are probably greater on the working-class than on the middle-class girl.[42] The working-class girl who aspires to a professional career is seen as especially threatening because her occupational aspirations (if achieved) would result in her being more successful than her father and brothers, in addition to being "unfeminine."

In contrast to lower-class white girls, lower-class black girls may have their educational and occupational aspirations actively supported by their families.[43] There is no difference in aspirations for boys and girls in intact black families, as there is in white families, and we have already noted Kandel's finding that black mothers in single-parent families had higher educational aspirations for their daughters than for their sons.[44]

White parents, in contrast, are more likely to "protect" their daughters and to hold them back, even when they think they are "helping" them. They may think they are treating their sons and daughters equally because they send them to the same schools, camps, etc., but the subtle messages they convey are different. For example, boys are typically allowed more freedom to play away from home, to return home later, and to choose their own activities.[45] As one of Komarovsky's students complained:

> My brother is 15, three years younger than I am. When he goes out after supper, mother calls out, "Where are you going, Jimmy?" "Oh, out." Could I get away with that? Not on your life. I would have to tell them in detail where to, with whom, and if I am half an hour late, mother sits on the edge of the living room sofa watching the door.[46]

Komarovsky concludes that the "risk of this kind of traditional upbringing resides in the failure to develop in the girl independence, inner resources, and that degree of self-assertion which life will demand of her."[47] Thus, both school and parents impede the growing girl's social and intellectual independence.

THE INFLUENCE OF PEERS

The equation of intellectual success with a loss of femininity appears to be common among high school peer groups. According to Keniston and Keniston, high school girls feel they must hide their intelligence if they are to be popular with boys.

> Girls soon learn that "popularity"—that peculiar American ecstasy from which all other goods flow—accrues to her who hides any intelligence she may have, flatters the often precarious maleness of adolescent boys, and devotes herself to activities that can in no way challenge their sex. The popular girls in high schools are seldom the brilliant girls; or if they are, it is only because they are so brilliant they can hide their brilliance from less brilliant boys. . . . Most American public schools (like many private schools) make a girl with passionate intellectual

interests feel a strong sense of her own inadequacy as a woman, feel guilty about these "masculine" outlooks, perhaps even wonder about her own normality.[48]

Thus, school, parents, and peers make it clear to girls that the major criterion for feminine success is attractiveness to men. Pierce found high achievement motivation for women related to success in marriage, not, as for males, to academic success.[49] In Pierce's view, girls see that to achieve in life they need to excel in nonacademic ways, i.e., in attaining beauty in person and dress, in finding a desirable social status, and in marrying the right man.[50]

The mass media reinforce this perception and provide explicit instruction on attaining these goals. *Seventeen, Glamour,* and *Mademoiselle* provide endless pages of fashion, make-up, and dating advice. The girl learns that she must know how to attract, talk to, kiss, keep (or get rid of) a boy, depending on the circumstances, and how to use clothes, cosmetics, and interpersonal skills to accomplish these all-important ends. While fashion magazines tell her how to dress, movies instruct on how to undress—and on the explicit use of sexuality. "On the whole, mass media and popular fiction continue to portray career women as mannish, loose, or both; and the happy ending for working girls still involves abandoning work, marrying, and having many children—and there the story ends."[51]

Just a decade ago one could summarize the three clear lessons that a well-socialized American girl had learned. One concerned her personality, the second her capability, and the third, her future role. With regard to her personality, she had learned to be nurturing, cooperative, sweet, expressive, not too intelligent, and fairly passive. With regard to her capability, she had learned she would always be less capable and less important than most men. With regard to her future, she had learned she would be a wife and mother, and, if she were successful, she would acquire that status soon. Today, as we shall see, the message has become much more complex for the middle-class college girl.

THE "TERMINAL YEAR" OF SCHOOL[52]

The end of high school is a critical juncture at which the lives of girls from lower- and middle-class families diverge. While many middle-class girls will go on to college, the last year in high school is what Sheila Tobias calls "the terminal year" for many lower class girls—their last year in school and their last chance "to find a husband." As Lillian Rubin's interviews with working-class girls reveals, for most of them "getting married was—and probably still is—the singularly most acceptable way out of an oppressive family situation and into a respected social status—the only way to move from girl to woman. Indeed, among working-class girls, being grown up means being married."[53]

Rubin accurately portrays the difference between the perspectives of working-class women and those from middle-class families:

> Among the [working-class] women, a few recall girlhood dreams of being a model or an actress, but most remember wanting only to marry and live happily ever after. . . . It's not that the girls from middle-class homes dreamed such different dreams. But along with the marriage fantasy, there was for them some sense of striving for their own development. Even if that were related to enhancing marriage prospects (that is, with a college education a girl can make a "better match"), some aspiration related to self existed alongside it. And, in fact, for those middle-class women, marriage came much later since it was (typically) deferred until after college.[54]

As Rubin notes, the terminal year for most middle-class girls doesn't come until the end of college (and for an increasing minority it doesn't come until the end of graduate school). But whenever it comes, it brings the same pressures to marry and settle down—to find a husband, to buy a home, to have children—and to fulfill one's role as "a woman."

Socialization

pressures

in college

Chapter 4

For a long time it seemed odd that young women who staunchly resisted the pressures to put social life and popularity above intellectual and vocational achievement during high school, suddenly changed during college. They switched their majors from Economics to English or Art History and decided they were not really interested in graduate school after all. What happened?

It now seems clear that what distinguished these college women from their working-class sisters was not a stronger commitment to intellectual pursuits, or to feminism, or to a non-traditional lifestyle, but the fact that they did not face the "terminal year" pressures until the end of college. For them the end of high school was just one more transition point. As long as they continued in school, they were permitted a moratorium on the pressures of "real life." But when these middle-class girls found themselves in their terminal year of college, and thus in the same structural position as their lower-class sisters at the end of high school, their behavior changed.

In the following discussion we shall describe the pressures on college women as if college were the terminal school for all middle-class women. However, women who go into professional or graduate school gain additional moratorium years and thereby further delay the pressures that come with the terminal year of school.

PEER INFLUENCES IN COLLEGE

It is now over 30 years since Mirra Komarovsky completed her classic study of sex role socialization of Barnard College women.[1] At that time (1946), college women reported that they felt caught between the traditional female role and the more modern role—and were constantly pressured by mutually exclusive expectations. For example:

> Uncle John telephones every Sunday morning. His first question is: "Did you go out last night?" He would think me a grind if I were to stay home Saturday night to finish a term paper. My father expects me to get an "A" in every subject and is disappointed by a "B." He says I have plenty of time for social life. Mother says, "That 'A' in Philosophy is very nice, dear, but please don't become so deep that no man will be good enough for you."[2]

One might speculate that women in college today are not being subjected to the same pressures. Although their parents may still encourage them to see marriage as the ultimate goal, it is possible that peer definitions of feminine roles are more liberal. The ideology of the current women's liberation movement certainly supports independent achievements for women.

In order to study this hypothesis (i.e., that college women are no longer subjected to anti-achievement pressures from peers) in a more systematic fashion, I decided to ask the students in my 1972 undergraduate course on the family (at the University of California at

49

Davis) to help me design a study. We decided to try a "field experiment," which involved the following procedure. Each of the students was to select a person of the opposite sex and sustain interaction with that person for at least one hour. During that hour, the student was to "act in accord with the ideals and goals of the women's liberation movement." (This experiment followed a class unit on the women's movement.) The choice of "feminist behavior" was left up to the individual student. The same procedure was repeated four years later, in 1976, with another undergraduate class on the family. Both classes had predominantly female enrollments.

Among the female students who completed the 1972 experiment, 27 percent reported a rejection of the feminist behavior by their male companion. In some cases these women were asked to change their behavior: "So after I told him why I was doing it, he said, 'Stop it, please, I don't want you to be a member of women's liberation.' " In other cases, the man treated the woman's ideas or actions as nonserious, tossing them off as a joke or "putting her down as crazy":

> I told him I thought being a housewife and a mother was a bore and a lot of shitwork. Well, this really got to him and he said I was crazy. . . . Just then his roommate came in and he related my "weird" ideas to him and they both had a good laugh.

> He said it wasn't a man's job to do the housework . . . and that any woman who had decided that she didn't want children was crazy.

In several instances, the friends and boyfriends were so angered or upset by the women's behavior that they refused to deal with it. They tried to terminate the interaction by telling the women they would never attract a man if they continued to act in such an unfeminine manner:

> He told me that if I wanted a man I should start acting like a woman because any man would ball me but if I wanted a husband I'd better do the right things.

In contrast to these emotional reactions, some of the men were more intellectual about their rejection, trying to answer the feminist arguments "rationally" by arguing that motherhood was fulfilling, or that a woman's career was too disruptive to a marriage:

> He said that if I went to law school I'd be challenging him at his own career and would be sacrificing our home life for a materialistic job. . . . He felt women with careers neglected their husbands and children and that they were basically selfish. . . . When I confessed that I was doing a class assignment he seemed relieved but later continued to discuss the disadvantages of a career for a woman.

The second most common reaction (17 percent) was that boyfriends or dates were merely surprised and uncomfortable:

> All of this made him feel uncomfortable, especially when I said this other guy had a good ass.

The third most common response, reported by 12 percent of the students, was subtle resistance by dates and male friends. Although not explicitly challenging the women, the men attempted to regain control of the situation:

> He asked if he could drive instead because he didn't like it to look as if he was being chauffeured around.

> I was sitting on the chair so he came over and handed me the broom, asking me to hold it, but really trying to put me into my proper role.

Most of these men denied trying to regain the dominant position in the relationship, contending that they were "just trying to be helpful."

> He asked how much the dinner cost and told me how much to leave for the tip.

Some of the women (8 percent) reported that their dates or boyfriends did not seem to resent their behavior, but other friends and observers did:

> The waiter seemed to feel sympathy for my boyfriend for being with such an assertive, pushy woman, while the cashier sided with me, assuming that by paying my share, I was being taken advantage of. She said sympathetically, "I've got one at home just like him."

These quotes indicate the extent to which third parties observe and try to reinforce conventional behavior, even when the couple is content with new roles.

In contrast to the reactions just described, some 10 percent of the women reported that the males they chose reacted positively to their behavior:

> He said he dug me in this particular role and that I should come across like that more often.

> He said he admired intelligent women who he could really talk to. . . .

> He said, "I'd rather have someone who would dig building a cabinet with me instead of worrying about ironing my shirts."

It is interesting to note that 27 percent of the women in the class found they could not carry out the assignment because acting liberated was so normal for them that none of their friends noticed any difference in their conversation or actions:

> Since this is the way I always act, no one reacted to anything I did.

> I rarely come into contact with people (especially men) who aren't in a liberated circle of people, and when I do, they don't have much to say.

If we combine this 27 percent of the students with the 10 percent who received positive reactions and the 8 percent who were hassled only by outsiders, we find that for almost half of the women in the first experiment group, there was positive peer support for rejecting the traditional feminine role. Thus, although a majority of these women university students were still being constrained by male peers to conform to more traditional standards of feminine behavior, change was also evident.

When I read the results of this study to my class in 1972, several students who had reported they received support for their actions said that this support had definite limits. Many had chosen "low-risk" situations for the class assignment—situations in which neither the man nor the woman had a great stake in the relationship and the woman's behavior was not of critical importance. Both these women and those who had characterized themselves as "already liberated" felt that when they were seriously involved with a man there were more pressures on them to play a more "feminine" role.

Other research on college women similarly suggests that the pressures for more traditional roles may grow especially severe during their junior and senior years in college or with involvement with a particular man. Horner's interviews with Radcliffe students show that parents and boyfriends exert great pressure on them to "return" to traditional feminine roles in their terminal year in the terminal school, and it is at this time that their intellectual performance usually drops.[3]

Another observation of the liberated women in my class was that expressions of peer support for their new role had been exaggerated. Although they themselves felt comfortable in the role, they reported encountering considerable problems in establishing relationships with men. Several felt they were no longer as attractive to men, or that most men did not know how to handle "the new women"— or preferred not to. As one woman reported, "I get a lot of support from both men and women, but most men say something like 'even though I'm really supportive of what you are, I just can't handle it. . . . I'm still hung up on having a more feminine woman who will support *me*'." Thus, although peers may appreciate the independence and intellectual companionship of the liberated woman, they may let her know that they do not consider her "a real woman."

The responses encountered by male students were much milder. On the whole, the men met much less resistance when they expressed and acted in accord with feminist ideals. Their responses were almost equally divided between no-response/normal response (36 percent), annoyance (30 percent), and approval (34 percent). In addition, even those who met "annoyance" reported it often seemed more a response to an unexpected situation than a strong disapproval of the behavior itself. For example, several males asked their dates to share the bill for a meal or to take them home. Most of the women agreed to these requests, and although they seemed annoyed not to have been asked in advance only two of them chided the men for being ungracious or "ungentlemanly."

The 1972 experiment did have one interesting side effect: one third of the men who did the assignment reported that the experience of articulating the arguments for women's liberation had a positive effect on them. One of them described it this way.

I think the most significant reaction was within myself. After discussing all the points that were made in class, I became more of a feminist. I think I convinced her about the movement, but I also convinced myself.

When I repeated this experiment with my undergraduate family class in 1976, both they and I were astonished by how much had changed. The majority of the class reported not only that they were unable to carry out the assignment (because their behavior now seemed "normal"), but they even had difficulty trying to "provoke" a reaction. Some attributed the lack of peer reaction to an increased tolerance for "doing one's own thing." Others, however, felt that a radical change in attitudes had resulted in genuine widespread support for the "new woman."

We will now examine the role expectations for this "new woman."

INTELLECTUAL ACHIEVEMENT: THE CLIMATE OF NON-EXPECTATION?

College should present an opportunity for women to broaden their intellectual horizons and to acquire both the background and motivation for occupational success. But in the past women have received less encouragement than men. Women professors have been underrepresented on the faculties of all colleges and universities in the United States, even in fields that were sex-stereotyped as female (such as English or Art History), and women received no more than a passing mention in the intellectual content of most courses.

The predominantly male faculty typically assumed that women came to college to find husbands and become well-rounded individuals. Few professors took their intellectual or occupational aspirations seriously.* As Paula Bunting, the former President of

---

*As psychologists Huston-Stein and Higgins-Trenk observe: "In the college years, individual

Radcliffe College observed, in her day the college environment for even the brightest women was one of "non-expectations." Instead of stimulating the bright young woman's intellectual and political ambitions, college worked as a depressant. Thus many college women came to believe they were less intelligent (or less brilliant or less creative) than their male peers. English Professor Florence Howe describes the internalized inferiority among the women in her creative writing seminar in the 1960s:

> What I learned from listening to my women students was that they consistently considered women writers (and hence themselves) inferior to men. . . . Why should naturally inferior writers attempt anything ambitious? . . . Their comments ranged from "I don't have any ideas" to "I can't write anything really interesting" to "I used to have ideas and imagination but I don't any more."[4]

Although the climate of non-expectations did not make all women doubt their own capacity, it inevitably had a depressant effect on their ambitions. Even those who began college with high aspirations found their expectations for themselves lowered by the time they were ready to graduate: Perhaps they should apply for an M.A. program instead of trying for a Ph.D., or perhaps they should take a year off and decide what they "really" wanted to do.

Even those who did well in school, and who therefore had the external validation of high grades, began to question whether they were "truly" as capable or as committed as their male peers. Of course, those women who got high grades had rarely received the kind of professional encouragement that was lavished on their male

---

encouragement by one or two faculty members is often an important impetus to high aspirations for women. At college graduation, career-committed women had more often worked with a professor in their field on independent study projects and more often felt that their professors considered them outstanding students. . . . [S]trong encouragement by one or two faculty members can be a critical determinant of the decision to pursue advanced professional status." Aletha Huston-Stein and Ann Higgins-Trenk, "Development of Females from Childhood through Adulthood: Careers and Feminine Role Orientations," in Paul B. Baltes, ed., *Life-Span Development and Behavior* (New York: Academic Press, 1978), p. 283

peers—a fact which could not have easily escaped their attention. Perhaps some of those male professors had really wanted to encourage their bright women students but feared their interest might be misinterpreted (by their colleagues or their wives, if not by their students). Others may have been concerned about dissuading women from what they thought was the woman's preferred life pattern, for it was widely assumed that women had to choose between a career and marriage.

In light of these expectations it is not surprising that women college students in the past have always been less likely to graduate from college than men, or that women college graduates have less often gone on to obtain advanced degrees.[5]

It is widely believed that the climate of expectations is quite different today. The data, however, are ambiguous. On one hand, there are several clear indications of change. In the years 1970 to 1976, for instance, there was a 30 percent increase in college enrollment of women compared with a 12 percent increase for men.[6] This indicates that the proportion of women seeking education beyond high school is fast approaching that of men.[7] In addition, more women are graduating from college and going on to obtain higher degrees. In 1971, women earned 42 percent of all BAs and 40 percent of all MAs.[8]

Women are also increasingly competing with men to gain entry into the high-prestige occupations that were traditionally closed to them.[9] The proportion of women enrolling in professional schools in law, medicine, engineering, and business has risen steadily since 1960. The percentage of women in medical schools grew from 6 percent of the total in 1960, to 13 percent in 1972, to 18 percent in 1974, and the percentage of women in law schools increased from 4 percent of the total enrollment in 1960, to 12 percent in 1972, to 19 percent in 1974.[10] Further, it is likely that the overall percentage of women in law will continue to rise because women currently make up 25 percent to 33 percent of the students in the first-year class at many of the better law schools.

Another indication of progress is the number of women awarded doctoral degrees. More women are now enrolled in graduate schools than ever before, and more of them are being awarded PhDs.

"Although women constitute only 14 percent of all PhDs awarded in 1971, that number is likely to rise quickly in the next few years, for the pool of candidates from which they are drawn is growing rapidly (both in actual numbers and compared with men.)"[11]

On the other hand, these statistics still reflect a difference in the climate of expectations for male and female students. As long as women constitute far less than 50 percent of the PhD candidates, medical students, and law students, it means college women still are not choosing and pursuing careers in the high-level professions *to the same extent* as their male peers.

It is also widely believed that college women today are much more career-oriented than the women who were in college in the 1950's and 1960's. But once again the data are unclear, for while the majority of college women now assume they will be employed in the future, their attitudes toward work and family roles suggest that many of them are still thinking in terms of "jobs" rather than "careers." The distinction between a job orientation and a career orientation is one that sociologist Alice Rossi has pinpointed as a critical difference between college men and women in the past.[12] She notes that even though college-educated women might study and prepare for a future occupation, they viewed these occupations as "jobs," not as lifelong vocational commitments. Their middle-class brothers, in contrast, were clearly future oriented, preparing and planning for lifelong careers. (Of course the women's lack of preparation for a lifelong career did not prevent them from working. It did, however, prevent them from organizing their lives for a "career" instead of a "job.")

Elizabeth Douvan has suggested that unmarried college women hold their identities in abeyance, lest premature identity formation reduce their marriage prospects or inhibit their ability to adapt to marriage.[13] It is possible that college women similarly hold back from making lifelong career plans because they expect their careers to be heavily influenced by their future husbands and their family life. If this is so, then the recent upsurge in college women who plan to combine marriage and work does not indicate a fundamental change in women's career orientation. For as long as a woman's work is contingent upon her marriage, or her husband, or her childbearing plans, she is still adhering to women's traditional priorities.

While it was formerly assumed that women had to choose between marriage and work, most college women today plan to combine the two. The shift in attitudes is striking in Cross's data on incoming freshmen women (in one college) between 1964 and 1970. The women were asked what they would like to be doing in fifteen years.[14] In 1964, 65 percent said they would like to be a housewife and mother. Since then, the percentage who express this desire has declined steadily each year—to 60 percent in 1966, to 53 percent in 1967, and to only 31 percent by 1970. In contrast, the percentage who say they want to be a married career woman has doubled; it rose from 20 percent in 1964 to 40 percent in 1970.

Several other studies of college women today confirm that an increasing number plan to combine marriage, family, and a career. In two recent studies, Cummings and Parelius found that almost all students at two women's colleges said they would like to combine the goals of marriage, family, and a career.[15]

Although the word *career* in these studies may not refer to the lifelong commitment we discussed above, it is clear that the new ideal for college women has become a life of both marriage and work. In addition, this appears to be the preferred life style for at least half of the adult women in the United States. A 1974 Roper poll found that over 50 percent of all adult women in the United States favored combining "marriage, children, and careers" and a 1975 Gallup poll found that 45 percent of women eighteen to twenty-four chose as "the most interesting and satisfying life for [me] personally" the option of "married, children, full-time job."[16]

Despite the widespread acceptance of employment for married women, it is useful to explore two ways in which the college woman's traditional socialization may create barriers to her occupational advancement. The first is the psychological fear that if a woman is too achieving or too successful she will not be regarded as feminine and will be rejected by men. The second is the cultural imperative that career women must still "prove" their femininity by being good mothers and wives and by not exceeding their husband's status and achievements.

FEAR OF SUCCESS

Matina Horner's famous experiment on fear of success was conducted in 1965.[17] Horner argued that for women, the desire to achieve is often contaminated by "the motive to avoid success" or the fear that success will have negative consequences.[18] This fear arises because women equate success with masculine achievement, and therefore with a loss of femininity.[19] They worry that they will be less feminine if they strive for success, and this anticipated consequence sets up a conflict that prevents them from achieving. Horner labeled this conflict "fear of success."[20]

In her first experiment Horner asked 90 female undergraduates to write a story when presented with the verbal cue, "After first-term finals, Anne finds herself at the top of her medical school class." Eighty-eight men were asked to respond to the same sentence, with the name John substituted for the name Anne. While the men were comfortable with John's success and saw a flourishing career and happy life ahead for him, the women associated Anne's success with social rejection. They predicted that she would be unpopular, unmarried, and lonely. The women's stories also portrayed Anne as unfeminine. They predicted that she would have doubts about both her femininity and her normality and finally, she would feel guilty and despairing for having achieved too much.

Horner concluded that most college women, consciously or unconsciously, equated intellectual achievement with loss of femininity. In testing and other achievement situations they were caught in a double bind, worried not only about failure but also about success.[21] "Thus women who were otherwise motivated to achieve, experienced anxiety in anticipation of success and this may have adversely affected their performance and levels of aspiration."[22]

In a second experiment Horner compared the students' performance on tests when they worked alone or in a competitive group. She found that "a large number of men did far better when in competition than when they worked alone."[23] Women who were rated low on fear of success behaved like the men. However, those women who showed high fear of success (77 percent) did better on a comparable task when they worked alone than when they worked in competition with others, and their performance deteriorated most noticeably in competition with men. Horner concluded that anxiety about success blocks achievement for many bright women.

As Tavris and Offir tell the story, "When Horner published her work, a chorus of 'Aha's!' went up throughout the land."

> Researchers thought they now understood why women had been ruining their studies. College women had a reason for their uncertain career plans. Journalists announced that an explanation had been found for women's low status in the world of work; the fault lay not in the stars but in women themselves. They might want to achieve, but they also wanted to be feminine, and the two motives were as incompatible as oil and water.[24]

Horner's research has since been widely replicated in a series of studies both in this country and elsewhere.* These studies show a remarkable range of results. For example, after a review of the recent literature, Tresemer reported that in 45 experiments which used women subjects, the proportion of women who wrote fear-of-success themes varied from 11 percent to 88 percent, with a median of 47 percent.[25] Tresemer also noted that recent experiments reveal college men, too, fear success. Among men, however, the fear relates to doubts about the value of conventional career goals. Men wonder whether hard work really pays off, in either college or career. (John may drop out of medical school to write a novel, or may hate being a doctor and wonder what it was all for, or may think "It's great for his parents, but he doesn't give a shit."[26]) Anne worries about becoming unpopular and dateless, but John worries about prematurely dropping dead.[27]

One recent interpretation of fear of success views it as a reflection of social reality rather than a deep-seated fear of achievement. Condry and Dyer suggest the analogy of asking people to write a story about an interracial couple who have just been married and are about to set up housekeeping in rural Georgia. Here, it would obviously

---

*For a good review of the literature see Martha Mednick, Sandra Tangri, and Lois Hoffman, eds., *Women and Achievement* (New York: John Wiley and Sons, 1975); John Condry and Sharon Dyer, "Fear of Success: Attribution of Cause to the Victim," *Journal of Social Issues*, 32, 3 (Summer 1976), 63-83; and David Tresemer, "Fear of Success: Popular, but Unproven," *Psychology Today*, 7 (March 1974), 82-85.

be wrong to label every story that mentions negative consequences as "fear of interracial marriage." "The people who predicted bad things for the couple would not necessarily be afraid or bigoted; they might just know which way the racist wind blows."[28] Thus, the stories about Anne and John may not reflect individual motives as much as they reflect "realistic assessments of the consequences of conforming or not conforming to social convention."[29]

Other critiques of Horner's studies question whether fear-of-success motives affect actual performance. As Tresemer points out, the women in Horner's group who were most likely to show fear of success were honors students. "If the people who show fear of success imagery are the ones who get good grades," he says, "just how deeply debilitating is it?"[30]

Whether or not fear of success reflects personal motivation or social reality, and whether or not it affects actual performance, I believe that if it presently exists at all it is a temporary phenomenon that will soon disappear. When young women are afforded more successful role models and more opportunities to observe how much fun (and power and money) success brings, they will rapidly lose any anxiety they have about it. Furthermore, in contrast to the current stereotype of successful women as unfeminine, I think young women will begin to discover that "success is sexy"—it increases rather than decreases one's attractiveness to the opposite sex. Just as in the past many women have been attracted to powerful men (even though they were not necessarily "handsome") it is likely that in the future more men will find dynamic and powerful women attractive.

Nevertheless, the continued anxiety that many college women currently associate with success suggests that the ideal of the wife-mother-career woman is not without its own anxiety. Furthermore, this anxiety may be exacerbated by cultural pressures on the career woman to prove that she is also a good wife and mother.

THE CULTURAL IMPERATIVES

The college woman who aspires to a successful career faces two cultural imperatives to prove that she is also a successful woman: one is to bear children; the other, to make sure her occupational achievements do not exceed those of her husband.

Because the belief that the successful career woman is unfeminine is widespread among both men and women,[31] career-oriented women may feel under particular pressure to prove their femininity. Lois Hoffman suggests that having a baby may provide the proof the career woman feels she needs.[32] (It may also force her to devote a great deal of time and energy to family roles and thereby reassert their priority in her life.) In a 1971 study of undergraduate women at the University of Michigan, Hoffman's question "What is the most womanly thing you can imagine?" most often elicited the response, "To have a baby."[33]

In view of this response, it is not surprising to find that several studies of women in the professions indicate that women in more masculine fields (law, medicine, and the hard sciences), women facing the strongest pressures to prove their femininity, tend to express a desire for more children than women in more conventionally feminine fields (the arts, humanities, education, and nursing.[34]). However, if motherhood solves one set of anxieties, its demands, especially in large families, may easily create other pressures and role conflicts for the young career woman.

A second cultural imperative is that wives should not exceed their husband's status and occupational attainment.[35] In fact, Hoffman suggests that for educated women a successful marital relationship often requires that both partners perceive the husband to be the more intelligent or successful in his career.[36] As Hoffman notes:

> any change in this perception may be a threat to the husband's sense of masculinity, the wife's sense of femininity, and thus to the love relationship. In many cases this threat may come simply from a change in the established equilibrium, such as when the career-wife has a success experience, or her husband has a failure; or when the nonworking wife considers returning to a career or seeking further education.[37]

How can the new woman balance these cultural imperatives with the demands of a career? How can she be and do everything?

One way to resolve the conflict is to have a clear sense of priority. Women's socialization suggests that they should treat work as a "job" and put their responsibilities to husband and family first. Is this what college women are choosing to do?

The limited data on occupational aspirations, career decisions, and dual-career marriages suggest that the majority still are.[38] And the pressure to continue to do so comes from their husbands, for changes in male expectations about women's roles appear to be lagging far behind women's aspirations. Most college men still want their wives to put husband and family first.[39] As Komarovsky's interviews with college men reveal, very few want their wives to work continuously or express any willingness to alter their own lives or careers to provide work opportunities for their wives.[40] Most prefer that she remain out of the labor force entirely until their children have completed school. A large number do not want their wives to work outside the home at any time, while the majority do not want her to work after her children are born. Thus, as Huston-Stein and Higgins-Trenk have noted, "Although many men want an intellectually equal companion with her own interests and talents, few seem aware of the need for such women to have a career rather than an occasional job, and most do not recognize the difficulties inherent in long interruptions of a career.[41]

Nor do the majority of college women seem to recognize the disruptive effects of an interrupted career pattern. In recent years most college women have said they plan a career with some years spent at home when children are young.[42] For example, in one college where women students were interviewed in both 1950 and 1971, only 20 percent expected to pursue a continuous career, usually in combination with marriage.[43]

Are all college women conforming to these pressures to put their husbands and families first? No, not all. Sociologist Laurie Cummings has found that a minority are beginning to organize their lives differently. Cummings set out to examine the differences among college women who aspired to combine marriage, motherhood, and work. She found that women who are feminists not only express greater confidence in their ability to combine job, family, and marriage, they also make more concrete plans for achieving their aims. They are more likely to plan to go to graduate school, to plan a continuous rather than an interrupted career.[44] They also

63

seem to have clearer ground rules for an egalitarian marriage. For example, Cummings discusses their responses to the question "How do you feel about women who work to put their husbands through school? Under what circumstances would you be willing to do this?"

> The least feminist women tend either to reject or accept the proposal about putting their husbands through school. . . . The most feminist women were more likely than the other groups to talk about the conditions for considering it. For instance, most either said they would support their husband if he would do the same for them or if it did not interfere with their own plans. In this respect there is evidence that their expectations and ideas of marital and familial duties differ from those of the less feminist women, just as their ideas about a career differ. The more feminist women have some sense of their ground rules for an egalitarian marriage; their answers suggest that they have certain *quid pro quo* established from which they would bargain.[45]

NEW DEMOGRAPHIC TRENDS

Despite the persistence of the cultural imperatives for most women, three demographic trends may be creating structural pressures for women to become more career oriented, whether they "intend" it or not. These trends are encouraging women who enter the labor force before marriage to stay there, and the longer women stay in the labor force the more likely they are to "get hooked" on work.

The three critical demographic trends are toward marrying later, postponing childbearing within marriage, and having fewer children.[46] When young women postpone marriage and childbearing within marriage, "they experience a relatively long period of time after completing high school or college during which they may advance in their careers."[47] This work experience increases their career involvement. Even women who enter work with no firm commitment to it commonly find their involvement increases over time.[48] And the longer they remain in the labor force, the more difficult it becomes for them to give up the benefits it confers in terms of income, economic independence, recognition, sense of achievement, and challenge.

In addition, the family of the working woman comes increasingly to rely on her salary, for a family accustomed to a two-income level of living is loath to abandon one leg of its support (especially in periods of inflation).[49] This creates another structural pressure for women to remain in the labor force.

The greater the rewards women receive from work the more likely they are to postpone childbearing, and the longer the period before childbearing the more their work orientation is strengthened. In addition, women who postpone childbearing are likely to have fewer children, and fewer children make it easier for mothers to remain in the labor force even when their children are young. (Today, over one third of all women with preschool children are in the labor force, in contrast to 12 percent in 1950.[50]) This pattern of continuous labor force participation creates, in turn, another "structural inducement" for more serious career commitments. An uninterrupted work history means that a worker can acquire more experience. This often leads to more job opportunities, which in turn leads to higher wages and more psychic satisfaction from work, which in turn leads to an increased commitment to work.*

While it is possible for women to continue to view these commitments as "job" commitments rather than "career" commitments, it is easy to see how structural factors might increasingly undermine that definition. In addition, a continuous work history, higher wages,

---

*Of course the opposite cumulative pattern also operates. As Huston-Stein and Higgins-Trenk observe: "the 'timing' of marriage, childbearing, education, and work have long-term implications for the life patterns of women. At one extreme, the probability of thwarted education and poverty accompanying adolescent motherhood is very high. . . . Once a choice is made, particularly having a child, the range of options becomes more limited, or at least some become more difficult to pursue. Although the majority of college women now anticipate both a career and marriage, they are often unrealistic about the difficulties of combining child rearing with a career (S. A. Shields, *Personality Trait Attribution and Reproductive Role*, M. A. Thesis, Pennsylvania State University, Department of Psychology, 1973). Many may make choices affecting their future life patterns without adequate understanding of the implications of those decisions." Aletha Huston-Stein and Ann Higgins-Trenk, "Development of Females from Childhood through Adulthood: Careers and Feminine Role Orientation," in Paul B. Baltes, ed., *Life-Span Development and Behavior* (New York: Academic Press, 1978), p. 278.

and increased work satisfaction should provide women with more ammunition to demand the *quid pro quo* that Cummings' feminist women seek to establish in their marriages.

The interaction

of socialization

influences: the case

of mathematics

Chapter 5

Although the previous discussion has focused on each aspect of the socialization process separately, in reality the influence of school, peers, and parents are interactive, and they support and reinforce each other. It is useful to focus on one specific area of education to illustrate this interactive process. I have chosen mathematics for this case study because of its vital role as a "critical filter" in the selection of college majors. Most of the college majors that readily lead to prestigious occupations—in medicine, chemistry, physics, engineering, computer science, architecture, and even agriculture and business administration—require either college calculus or statistics. But few women have the high school math necessary to take these courses and few colleges offer compensatory math preparation. In 1972, sociologist Lucy Sells found that only 8 percent of the entering female students at the University of California at Berkeley had sufficient math prerequisites (4 years of high school math) to enable them to major in science, engineering, or any of the other math-based subjects.[1] In contrast, 57 percent of the entering male students had sufficient high school math. Thus the potential choice of majors and subsequent career opportunities of 92 percent of the women were severely limited by their lack of mathematical training.*

Let us begin with the question of whether or not there are sex differences in mathematical ability. While many researchers have investigated this subject, the results are mixed and non-conclusive. Further, as Professor John Ernest has observed, there is no consensus as to what "mathematical ability" is: some researchers measure computational proficiency, others geometric or algebraic aptitude, while the psychologists will usually measure some more precise and specific intellectual function.[2]

One comprehensive survey of research evidence on sex differences in math performance concludes that there are no clear findings: some studies show girls performing better; others, done with students at the same grade level, find boys doing equally well or better.[3] Although it may be premature to conclude that there are no sex differences in mathematical ability and performance, what seems clear in light of the contradictory evidence is that if ability differences do exist, they cannot be very strong. Nevertheless, girls seem to get the message that they do not have the same mathematical ability as boys. As a result, they have less confidence in their mathematical skills and screen themselves out of math courses. How do girls come to believe they have less mathematical ability?

Surprisingly, we find no sex differences in *liking* for arithmetic. In a 1973 study of students in grades 2 through 12, John Ernest and his colleagues at U.C. Santa Barbara found that although boys tended

---

*In October 1977 Sells replicated her study at the University of Maryland, surveying a stratified sample of incoming freshmen by race and sex. She found the proportions still much the same: 57 percent of the white males had four years of high school math; 20 percent of the black males; 15 percent of the white females (a slight improvement); and only 10 percent of the black females.

to prefer science and girls tended to prefer English, both boys and girls liked mathematics in equal proportions (about 30 percent of both sexes said it was their favorite subject; 24 percent liked it second best).[4]

This lack of sex difference in mathematics preference holds true up to the twelfth grade, although its popularity declines in the high school years for both boys and girls. Ernest concludes there is nothing intrinsic about math that makes it more appealing to one sex. Nevertheless, he assumes that boys take more mathematics courses "not for the superficial reason that they like mathematics more than women but because, whether they like it or not, they are aware that such courses are necessary prerequisites to the kinds of future occupations, in medicine, technology or science, they envision for themselves."[5]

Let us examine how parents, peers, and teachers influence this process. With respect to parents, Ernest found that both boys and girls get more help from their mothers with homework in all subjects until the sixth grade. But beginning in the sixth grade, the father helps more in mathematics. The father then is the "authority" on mathematics and continues this role through high school. This fact alone must have its subtle influence on a young girl's (or boy's) attitude.[6]

While peer group attitudes are "sex neutral" in the elementary school years (boys say that boys do better in all subjects while girls say that girls do better in all subjects), by high school a consensus emerges and more students say boys do better than girls in mathematics.[7] (Only 16 percent of all students thought girls did better; 52 percent thought there was no difference.)

Similarly, Lynn Fox, an educator who studied precocious math students for her doctoral thesis at Johns Hopkins University, found that "there are more negative stereotypes for math-gifted girls than boys." Further, mathematically apt girls "seem more willing to sacrifice intellectual stimulation to social stimulation."[8] Other studies have confirmed that girls' performance in math plummets at around age twelve when adolescence makes them more aware of social roles.[9]

Along the same lines, sociologist Sanford Dornbusch reports that when high school students were asked "When you get a poor grade, which reason do you think usually causes the poor grade?," most students gave lack of effort as the reason in every subject. However, when it came to math, 26 percent of the females gave lack of ability as the basis for a poor grade as compared to 15 percent of the males.[10] Female students in every ethnic group in San Francisco were more than three times as likely to say, "I'm not good in math" as the reason for a poor grade as "I'm good in math" as the basis for a good grade.[11] Further, Dornbusch reports, this pattern was found in no other subject for either males or females.

Elizabeth Fennema and Julia Sherman, who have studied how sexual stereotyping affects attitudes and proficiency in mathematics, conclude "there is, then, an accumulation of evidence which points to the conclusion that sexual stereotyping of mathematics as a male domain operates through a myriad of subtle influences from peer to parent and within the girl herself to eventuate in the fulfillment of the stereotyped expectation of a female head that's not much for figures."[12]

Sheila Tobias's book *Overcoming Math Anxiety,* has a section entitled "Street Mathematics," in which she suggests that in addition to negative reinforcement, girls miss learning mathematics naturally at play. For example, she observes that baseball calculations of runs batted in provide challenges in fractions, ratios, and percentages, and throwing and catching a ball involves visualizing a parabolic curve.[13] Similarly, handling a stopwatch or building and taking apart mechanical objects trains boys to think mathematically and, even more important, demonstrates the practical utility of mathematics.

Stereotyped attitudes of peers and students are reinforced by (and are also a result of) the messages they receive in school—both in textbooks and in the expectations of teachers. Weitzman and Rizzo have shown that the most widely used textbooks portray math as a masculine domain.[14] They found males outnumber females 3 to 1 in math textbook illustrations and many of the problems perpetuate extreme sex role stereotypes. For example, women are shown having trouble counting to three; girls are stereotyped in problems as "girls who cry"; and Alan earns more than Jane for doing the same hourly work.

With regard to teachers' expectations, Ernest reports that 41 percent of the elementary and high school teachers he interviewed felt that boys did better in mathematics, while none of them felt that girls did better.[15] Such expectations may eventually have a "Pygmalion effect"—that is, the student may perform much as the teacher expects. This creates a self-fulfilling prophecy in which those expected to do well perform as expected. Thus, if 41 percent of the teachers expect superior performance from boys, they may, in fact, help to create it. Conversely, however, when teachers expect female students to do poorly in math, they must accordingly affect the girls' performance,* or at least the girls' attitudes and expectations, as well.

For many girls, the result of all these socialization pressures— from peers and parents and teachers—is what Sheila Tobias has labeled "math anxiety."[17] According to Tobias, math anxiety is an

> "I can't" syndrome, and whenever it strikes—for some as early as sixth grade, with word problems; for others, with the first bite of algebra; for still others, not until calculus or linear algebra or statistics, after a high school record of achievement in mathematics—it creates the same symptoms and response. "I can't do this. No amount of practice or trying will make it work for me. I never really understood math. I always memorized and got away with it. Now I've hit the level I always knew was there. I can't do it."
>
> Once a person has become frightened of math, she or he begins to fear all manner of computations, any quantitative data, and words like "proportion," "percentage," "variance," "curve," "exponential."[18]

We began this section by pointing to mathematics as an example of the interactive and cumulative effect of pressures from peers, parents, and teachers—all pointing in the same direction, all telling girls that mathematics is a masculine domain. However, since all the socialization influences point in the same direction, a change in any

---

*Of course there is always the unusual girl who persists despite lack of encouragement. For example, a tiny survey conducted at Stanford revealed that women majoring in natural sciences, mathematics, and engineering had received less encouragement to pursue math studies than had any group of Stanford males, even those males who were majoring in history or the humanities.[16] These "exceptions" will be discussed in Chapter 6.

71

one of them could break the pattern of *consistent* reinforcement. Thus, encouragement from a single parent or teacher, or peer support from just one or two other "math freaks," could break the cycle.

One experimental study along these lines was conducted by Lynn H. Fox at Johns Hopkins University.[19] Fox worked on two experimental summer programs which allowed bright sixth grade students to take accelerated algebra. The first program was offered to both boys and girls. However, fewer girls than boys enrolled in the program, and those girls who did attend enjoyed the class less and accomplished less than the boys in the program. In fact, several girls who were making satisfactory progress wanted to drop the course because they did not like "competing with the boys."[20] Thus, although both the girls and the boys were chosen on the basis of their mathematical ability, their success with the program was quite different.

The second program attempted to create a special class that would appeal to girls. This class was limited to girls and was organized around small-group and individualized instruction. It was conducted informally, and cooperative rather than competitive activities were stressed. There were three women teachers who were expected to serve as role models, and whenever possible, the teachers emphasized ways in which mathematics could be used to solve social problems.[21] "The ultimate goal was to make the girls more self-sufficient in studying mathematics and to find the experience challenging and satisfying."[22]

Fox found that the girls who completed the second program were successful in learning algebra at a high level. By the end of the summer, eighteen of the girls in the experiment were ready to begin the study of Algebra II.

But the researchers were surprised to find that many of these girls subsequently encountered negative reactions at school. When they tried to enroll in Algebra II, nine of the eighteen discovered that their principal or guidance counselor was reluctant to place them in the class. Three of these girls were finally persuaded to repeat Algebra I, and one girl was placed on one-month probation in Algebra II. The remaining fourteen were officially enrolled for Algebra II, but a number of them were told they were not expected to perform well.

They were also warned that they would be back into Algebra I if they did not succeed quickly in the course. In fact, several counselors and teachers expressed negative feelings toward the program and told the girls not to come to them for help.[23] By the end of the first six weeks of school two more girls were transferred back into Algebra I and at the end of the first semester another two were put back. "Thus, out of eighteen girls who completed the program, only eleven girls (61 percent) were able to accelerate their progress in school."[24]

As Fox notes, "While it is difficult to believe that teachers would deliberately try to fail some of the girls . . . several parents reported that the schools were determined to get the girls out of Algebra II . . . and more than one reported that the teacher told the student that she didn't think the girl could possibly know algebra well enough after only three months of study to do well in Algebra II. Whether or not teachers or counselors did indeed intentionally fail some girls, it seems likely that such negative attitudes worked against the girls."[25]

Fox concluded that a major difference between the girls who were successful and those who were not, was in their reports about the attitude of teachers and school officials. While all the girls who were less successful reported problems with the school, only one of the successful girls reported having problems with her teacher and guidance counselor. In fact, the girls who were considered to be the very best students in their Algebra II class had teachers, counselors, and principals who were highly enthusiastic about the program and were pleased with the success of these girls.[26]

A more striking example of the impact of a single pro-math influence is provided by Professor Joan Birman of Barnard-Columbia:

> I learned last year, to my astonishment, that for about four years running, the honors calculus course had been all male, in spite of the fact that admission was based on an open competitive examination. This fall, one of the senior mathematics majors and myself made an intensive effort to encourage women to *try the exam!* The typical answer was, "I know I won't pass it,"—to which we replied over and over, "Well, if you try it, at worst you will confirm what you already know, and only an hour of time will have been lost." After three days of such

advising, the big day came, the exam was given, and this year the class has five men and five women![27]

Birman's experience suggests the powerful potential of a single contrary influence.* This insight leads directly to the next chapter, which examines how women have managed to achieve despite the socialization pressures we've discussed.

*Other intervention strategies, such as peer counseling (Mills College, Oakland, California), alternate math curricula for women students (Wellesley College), Math Anxiety Clinics (Wesleyan University, Connecticut), and Adult Group Therapy (Mind Over Math, New York City) operate on the same theoretical assumption. As Tobias states it, "Math anxiety is probably as much a result, as it is a cause of math avoidance in women and girls."[28]

The achievers:

where does

socialization fail?

LIBRARY
OF
MOUNT ST. MARY'S
COLLEGE
EMMITSBURG, MARYLAND

Chapter 6

Although this discussion has emphasized formal academic and occupational achievement throughout, it should be clear that there are other areas in which both men and women are motivated to achieve. For example, some people make lifetime careers of philanthropy or unpaid volunteer work. Some devote their energies to civic affairs. Others aspire to positions of responsibility in religious or recreational organizations. Still others undertake technical or creative pursuits such as photography, painting, weaving, or wine-making. Even when these activities bring no monetary return, they often give participants a sense of achievement and success.

Nonetheless, there are limits to the rewards that unpaid activities can bring in American society. In general we accord status on the basis of occupational and financial achievement. It is therefore useful to focus on these activities; and when we do it is clear that, after relentless conditioning of the kind we have just reviewed, women are not generally socialized to adopt the personality characteristics that are related to success in the more prestigious and financially lucrative occupations.

Yet it is equally clear that there are many significant exceptions to this generalization. Many girls somehow do not get the message that they are supposed to be less intelligent and less successful than boys until they reach high school,* and some manage to avoid it through their college years. Further, in spite of overwhelming pressures to conform to the traditional feminine role, many women aspire to intellectual and professional success, and a significant number of them attain it. How can we account for these women? Are they deviants, or have we presented an over-socialized portrait of women in this essay?

In the statistical sense, women who have attained professional success are deviants, in that they are distinctly in the minority; but it is important to realize what a significant minority they are. We have already noted the wide range of individual differences in both sexes and the extent to which our summary has excluded the statistical minority of woman achievers. In this chapter we shall focus on this "deviant" group, composed of female doctors, lawyers, engineers, architects, professors, scientists, corporation executives, writers, etc., and ask what has been different about the socialization of these women. The following discussion will, of necessity, be speculative, because there has not yet been a systematic study of the socialization of high-achieving women. It is meant to be suggestive.

FAMILY BACKGROUND

One might speculate on various family situations that would encourage a girl's occupational aspirations: being a successful businessman's only child, who has been encouraged to take over her family's

*This point was raised by Naomi Weisstein in "Kinder, Kuche, Kirche as Scientific Law," *Motive,* April 1969.

business; being the daughter of a female doctor, encouraged to assist in her mother's office; or being the oldest sibling in a large family for whom leadership and authority are natural. The possibilities for such special situations to arise are endless.

But in a more general vein, it seems obvious that mothers provide an important source of influence for the goals and ideals of their daughters. A mother's own life, her values, and her personal aspirations can do much to establish the framework from which the young girl views the world and its possibilities. Unfortunately, although the topic has long fascinated and engaged the attention of psychiatrists and novelists, we still know remarkably little about how mothers shape their daughters' life course, directly or indirectly, positively or negatively. Some of the literature suggests that occupationally successful mothers and mothers possessed of high achievement motivation provide positive models for their daughters. But the reverse has also been suggested—i.e., that whatever the achievement motivation of mothers, the daughters tend to assert a contrary orientation in an attempt to attain something different for themselves.

One line of research that has produced fairly consistent results has explored the relationship between mothers' employment history and their daughters' work orientation. In summarizing this literature, psychologists Huston-Stein and Higgins-Trenk note that "daughters of employed mothers (i.e., mothers who were employed during some period of the daughter's childhood or adolescence) more often aspire to a career outside the home, get better grades in college, and aspire to more advanced education.[1] These young women are likely to see employment as "natural" for a woman and to plan their own futures accordingly.

Hartley found that girls between the ages of eight and eleven had future plans that were significantly related to their mothers' work roles. When asked what they expected to do when they grew up, significantly more daughters of nonemployed mothers gave "housewife" as their primary choice.[2] In contrast, more of the daughters of working mothers envisioned themselves working, even after marrying and having children. In addition, they were more likely to mention nontraditional professional areas (such as medicine, law, creative work) as their vocational choices.[3]

77

Employed mothers also seem to communicate less stereotyped views of sex roles. When compared to daughters of homemakers, daughters of employed women expressed less stereotyped views of the feminine role and were more likely to choose a traditionally masculine occupation.[4] According to Huston-Stein and Higgins-Trenk, "The apparent modeling influence of an employed mother is not a recent phenomenon: it appears across age cohorts, and it appears for both children and adults."[5] In all these studies adult career women more often had mothers who were employed during their childhood than did comparable groups of homemakers.[6]

Traditional identification theory assumed that the same-sex parent was the more crucial in determining the sex role identity of the child. This theory, which grew out of Freudian theory, asserted that the child must, in order to identify properly as a member of his or her sex, have a same-sex model to imitate.[7] Thus by imitating the father the boy would learn and internalize masculine behavior. Similarly, it was assumed, the girl would learn how to be feminine by imitating the behavior of her mother. According to this theory, the child internalizes not only the particular behavior observed, but a complex integrated pattern of sex-related behavior.[8] I would suggest instead, that a large amount of sex role behavior can be learned only through interaction with the opposite sex. This is especially true of the "feminine role," which is often defined in terms of relationships with others. It is thus possible that the father teaches the girl how to be feminine as much as the mother does.

Identification theory may be challenged on another ground as well. Identification theorists have assumed that it is necessary for adult role models to have clearly differentiated sex roles, so that the child can clearly distinguish what is masculine and what is feminine behavior.[9] However, Slater has indicated that adult role models who exhibit stereotyped sex role identification may impede, rather than facilitate, the child's sex role identification. Children may find it easier to identify with less differentiated and less stereotyped parental role models.[10] It is more likely that they will internalize parental values when nurturance (the typically feminine role) and discipline (the typically masculine role) come from the same source.

Both of these challenges to traditional identification theory suggest that the father may play an equally important role in his daughter's sex role socialization. Earlier we suggested that fathers often play a more critical role than mothers in reinforcing sex role *stereotypes,* because fathers are more likely to want their daughters to be feminine, attractive, affectionate and socially acceptable. We now suggest that when fathers do not fit this typical pattern, when they encourage their daughters' achievements and back up their encouragement with practical support, they can provide the single vital influence that breaks the traditional socialization chain. Thus, while a father's encouragement is clearly not the only precursor to female achievement (and, in fact, women are less likely to have an encouraging father than an encouraging mother), when it does exist it can be extremely influential.

Although there are no directly supporting data, sociologist William J. Goode has speculated that one especially strong stimulus to female achievement motivation is the father who not only encourages his daughter, but also makes his love and approval dependent on her task performance.[11] He lets her know that he cares about her achievements and he rewards her when she achieves. This pattern differs from two more common patterns of father-daughter interaction. In one typical pattern, the father gives his daughter unconditional support and love no matter what she does—just because she is his daughter. In the second pattern, the father makes his love contingent upon his daughter's success *in feminine spheres*—that is, his love is given as a reward for her being attractive, sociable, helpful, and affectionate.

In contrast to both of these patterns, the pattern in which the father makes his love contingent upon his daughter's success in *nonfeminine spheres* may be the pattern that stimulates the highest achievement in women. The father who indicates that he considers his daughter's achievement important and who encourages her to achieve for him—and for his love—encourages her as well to strive for success itself. This hypothesis has its parallel in research on male achievement motivation, where McClelland's work has shown that a strong mother-son relationship (in which the mother makes her love and approval conditional on her son's success) is most conducive to masculine achievement motivation.[12]

Heilbrun has shown, in fact, that highly successful girls tend to have an especially close relationship with, and to identify with, a masculine father.[13] This kind of relationship can be a great spur to "masculine" achievement, especially when there are no sons in the family or when the father for some other reason particularly supports and assists his daughter's aspirations. Some research indicates that an achievement-encouraging father is likely to have high occupational status. Having achieved himself, he is willing to encourage achievement in his daughter, particularly when she is his oldest child (or when he has no son).[14] A number of successful women appear to have been their father's "favorite" child and were encouraged to think of themselves as his prime successor. The role and influence of fathers, then, like that of mothers, is a fascinating topic that is open to future research.

THE OVERSOCIALIZED PORTRAIT OF WOMEN

Thus far, we have considered high occupational achievement and achievement motivation in women as if it were deviant, and therefore required a "special" explanation. However, an alternative view suggests instead that *most women are motivated to achieve*. This perspective would lead one to suspect that much of the literature reviewed in this book exaggerates the cumulative effectiveness of sex role socialization. In fact, because we have focused on averages, we have discussed sex role socialization as if its messages were generally accepted. As a result, we have presented an oversimplified, oversocialized portrait of both women and men.

If we now re-evaluate the socialization literature reviewed in this book from a more critical perspective, we can pinpoint five ways in which the literature exaggerates the effectiveness of the socialization process:

1. It is assumed that socialization is a consistent process.
2. It is assumed that sex role socialization is unidimensional in its behavioral effects.
3. It is assumed that the well-socialized woman has accepted and internalized the feminine role.
4. It is assumed that socialization fosters imitative behavior.

5. It is assumed that socialization ends with formal education, and thereafter one's personality and future course are "fixed."

Let us examine each of these assumptions.

The first way in which the socialization literature incorrectly portrays the socialization process is that it presents socialization as a consistent process. Thus it is assumed that women are consistently rewarded for feminine behavior and consistently punished for or discouraged from unfeminine behavior. Social learning theory, which is the basis for the bulk of the material presented in this book, holds that sex-appropriate responses are consistently rewarded and reinforced—and sex-inappropriate behavior consistently discouraged or punished—in the young girl until she comes to learn and internalize the feminine role.[15]

Without denying the pressures on women to conform to the feminine role, one can see that women are socialized in an ambivalent or *contradictory* fashion. At the same time that girls are rewarded for typical feminine behavior, they are also rewarded for some types of "masculine" behavior. This is because what is labeled masculine behavior is generally highly regarded and rewarded in our society. The girl who excels in school, wins the tennis championship, or fixes a broken car receives approval for each of these activities. Although she may be regarded as too aggressive or masculine, she is also admired for her accomplishments. Thus, the feminine role is not consistently reinforced.

A second fallacy in the socialization literature is what we referred to in Chapter 2 as the "unidimensional fallacy." When we examined the literature on black women we noted that since many people have some "masculine" traits and some "feminine" traits, and since many of our sex-typed behaviors are situationally specific, it is erroneous to think of individuals as *either* masculine *or* feminine. For example, Tobias notes that women who succeed in math and science, and who therefore might be considered most "deviant" of all, do not score low on *all* feminine characteristics, but only on those feminine characteristics that are inappropriate to their own individual self-image. They are "aggressive" (not passive), but they are also "nurturant" and "caring" (not "cold" and "aloof").[16]

81

Further, Potter found that the women with higher math ability responded positively to a cluster of attributes considered masculine, such as "logical," "persistent" and "intellectual." But this group also scored high on positively-valued feminine attributes, such as "warm," "generous" and so on. What these women seemed to be rejecting, the researcher concluded, was not femininity itself, but the low-valued feminine characteristics such as dependency and passivity. They seemed to have a healthy orientation toward the best of both the male and female worlds.[17]

Similarly, in a study of successful adolescent women, Heilbrun found the subjects both instrumental and expressive; that is, they exhibited the goal-directedness of typically successful males as well as the interpersonal sensitivity of typically successful females.[18] So long as the scoring of sex role identities is done on an either-or basis, or the "masculine" choices are tallied against the "feminine" choices, these multifaceted combinations of the traits of both sexes are easily overlooked.

A third problem in the socialization literature is that it assumes that women typically internalize the feminine role and derive pleasure, happiness, and satisfaction from it. They enjoy baking fresh cookies for their children, are fulfilled by the use of their administrative talents in running their households, and are gratified when their behind-the-scenes efforts help their husbands and children to achieve in the outside world. Thus it is assumed that women who have been successfully socialized have internalized the feminine role and are satisfied with it. If this were so, then the women who most closely conform to the ideal female role, i.e., the housewives, should be the most contented women. However, housewives seem to be less happy and less fulfilled than their employed counterparts: almost every study of women's fulfillment has shown that the women who most embrace the traditional feminine role are the least satisfied with their lot.[19] After reviewing the literature on feminine happiness and fulfillment, both Jessie Bernard[20] and Betty Friedan[21] concluded that most women simply are not content with that traditional role.

A fourth difficulty in the socialization literature is that it has probably overestimated the extent to which the socialization process fosters imitative behavior. For example, it is assumed that when children see girls rewarded for attractiveness and helpfulness and boys rewarded for initiative and independence in picture books, textbooks, and movies or on television, they will then pattern their behavior after these models. Granted, this inference appears plausible, but the cause-and-effect relationship has never been proven. While many girls will in fact treat the female characters as models, others may write them off as unattractive or unreal, and still others may identify with the male characters. This variation in reactions should lead future researchers to question the assumed success of the socialization process—and to try to investigate when and under what conditions it does affect behavior. For now, however, it seems likely that the socializing influence of the media has been exaggerated.

The same caveat should be applied to the socializing influence of parents, teachers, and peers. For example, it has been assumed that if parents or teachers or significant peers communicate sex-stereotyped expectations, boys and girls will conform to these expectations. Here again, while this may be true on the average, no one has yet established a clear cause-and-effect relationship. In addition, there are many areas in which we already know that an "expected behavior" commonly does not occur. (For example, in discussing "fear of success" we noted that girls manifesting the most fear of success were honors students.) Thus while it is likely that most women will not excel in the absence of supportive parents or teachers or peers, some obviously will—and do—and, in fact, some seem to positively thrive on the challenge posed by a disparaging parent, teacher, or friend.

A fifth and final inaccuracy in the socialization literature is that it seems to take for granted the notion that socialization takes place only when one is young. It assumes that when one's formal education is complete (whether it be at the high school or college level or at the end of professional school or training), one's personality and life course are irrevocably "fixed."

We need not look far for evidence to refute this notion, for it is becoming increasingly clear that the process of education and development continues throughout the life cycle. Even for one who clings to the idea that socialization is necessarily linked to formal education (a dubious assumption), a look at the changing pattern of education in recent years will encourage a "life course" perspective. For example, the college enrollment of women between twenty-five and thirty-four years of age increased 102 percent between 1970 and 1974 (from 409,000 per year to 831,000).[22] In fact, women in this age group now constitute one-fifth of the population of college women.[23]

These "older" women are likely to be re-entry women—women who have married and had children. As Van Dusen and Sheldon note, such women reflect two of the biggest changes in the life cycle of American women: changes in marital and childbearing patterns that have made continuing education easier to arrange, and changes in the labor market that have enhanced the desirability of acquiring that education.[24] These new outlooks mean that "those women *not* in the traditional student cohort—those who are older, who are married, or who have children—are no longer deemed to have 'missed the boat' by having taken on family roles before completing their schooling."[25] While obviously not all women will decide to return to school, those who do undoubtedly will be subjected to a new set of socialization influences and it is virtually certain that as a result they will develop and change.

To date, these developing trends toward midlife resocialization experiences have received little research attention. Also neglected are most of the socialization experiences that occur in the course of everyday life in the middle and advanced years. As Huston-Stein and Higgins-Trenk observe, we need to study how a person changes "as a result of staying home as a housewife and mother for several years . . . [or] as a result of engaging in a particular kind of job."[26]

One type of extra-educational socialization experience that has received some attention is "the midlife crisis." The literature suggests that midlife crises are often followed by periods of dynamic growth and development.[27] While most of this literature focuses on men, it seems plausible to surmise that women undergo some parallel experiences after midlife crises. The data on divorced women are suggestive here and seem to support the notion of growth after radical midlife change. Studies of women who re-enter college or graduate school after a divorce indicate that they are likely to be serious about their work, to earn high grades, to be career-oriented, and to work continuously after graduation. For example, in a nationwide sample of 33,000 graduate students Feldman found that divorced women were more committed to graduate school and careers than either married women or other single women, "despite the fact that almost 70 percent of them had at least one child."[28] While this does not mean that all life crises will have positive effects or will be followed by periods of new growth and development,* it does suggest that they are likely to trigger new socialization change—and that they deserve more attention as socialization influences in midlife.

THE NEED FOR STRUCTURAL CHANGE

If we are correct in asserting that the socialization of women into the traditional female roles is neither totally effective nor totally consistent, then one might legitimately ask why there are not more visible examples of high-achieving women. If, as we have asserted, many women are actually motivated to higher achievement, why has the proportion of women in the professions and in other high-status occupations remained so low?

There are two possible answers to this question. The first is that women's achievement is channeled in a different direction. As noted above, Pierce has shown that women with high achievement motivation are oriented toward finding high-status husbands.[29] Tobias suggests that the women who graduated in the 1950's married the men they themselves wanted to be.[30] Press and Whitney and Lipman-Blumen have also hypothesized that women see success in terms of heterosexual relationships, and that they attain vicarious gratification from the achievements of their husbands and sons.[31] In fact, Press and Whitney suggest that women with high achievement motivation pick males who will succeed, so that they may experience success vicariously.[32]

But even though women have been socialized to regard personal

---

*In fact, Feldman's research suggests that divorced male graduate students feel more burdened and strained than their male colleagues. In contrast, divorced female students feel freer to pursue their education. Saul D. Feldman, "Impediment or Stimulant? Marital Status and Graduate Education," in J. Huber, ed., *Changing Women in a Changing Society* (Chicago: University of Chicago Press, 1973), p. 231.

occupational success as difficult or undesirable, it seems unlikely that many women with high achievement motivation would be content with vicarious achievement alone. Unless they are allowed to play a significant role in their husbands' or sons' careers, they are likely to channel their energies elsewhere. It is obvious that the energies of many capable women are channeled into volunteer work or into other nonremunerative pursuits. Other high-achievement-oriented women may be found in frustrating jobs that are much below their capability, or in positions that involve power and capabilities that are neither recognized nor rewarded (with either money or position) by their employers.

A second answer to the question of why there are not more visible examples of high-achieving women lies in the structural opportunities available to women in this society. When women are denied real opportunities for advancement and are discriminated against at every stage of the process leading to a professional position, it is not surprising that they have not "made it." Thus, the answer to this question probably lies not so much in the socialization of women as in the structural opportunities available to them in our society.

As long as women are denied real career options, it is realistic for them not to put all their energy into occupational goals. As long as they lack role models of successful career women, are denied structural supports to aid a career, are told they are neurotic or unfeminine if they are dedicated to an occupation, we cannot expect large numbers of young women to aspire to professional careers. The major way to change their (accurate) perceptions about future options is to create *real options* for them.

Notes

NOTES TO INTRODUCTION

1. Margaret Mead, *Sex and Temperament in Three Primitive Societies* (New York: Morrow, 1939; Mentor Books, 1950).

2. Michelle Zimbalist Rosaldo, "Women, Culture and Society: A Theoretical Overview," in Michelle Zimbalist Rosaldo and Louise Lamphere, eds., *Woman, Culture, and Society* (Stanford, Calif.: Stanford University Press, 1974) p. 18.

3. John Money and Anke A. Ehrhardt, *Man and Woman and Boy and Girl* (Baltimore, Md.: The Johns Hopkins University Press, 1972); John Money, *Sex Research: New Developments* (New York: Holt, Rinehart, 1965); "Sex Hormones and Other Variables in Human Eroticism," in William C. Young, ed., *Sex and Internal Secretions*, 3rd ed., vol. 2 (Baltimore: Williams and Wilkins, 1961), pp. 1383-1400; and John L. Hampson and Joan Hampson, "The Ontogenesis of Sexual Behavior in Man," in *ibid.*, pp. 1401-32.

1. Mirra Komarovsky, *Women in the Modern World* (Boston: Little, Brown, 1953).

2. Jeffrey Z. Rubin, Frank J. Provenzano, and Zella Luria, "The Eye of the Beholder: Parents' Views on Sex of Newborns," *American Journal of Orthopsychiatry,* 44, 4 (1974), 512-19.

3. *Ibid.*

4. *Ibid.,* p. 519.

5. Jerrie Will, Patricia Self, and Nancy Datan, unpublished paper presented at 82nd annual meeting of the American Psychological Association, 1974, as cited in Carol Tavris and Carole Offir, *The Longest War: Sex Differences in Perspective* (New York: Harcourt Brace Jovanovich, 1977).

6. Tavris and Offir, *The Longest War,* p. 173.

7. Howard A. Moss, "Sex, Age, and State as Determinants of Mother-Infant Interaction," *Merrill-Palmer Quarterly,* 13, 1 (1967), 19-36, 28, 30.

8. *Ibid.*

9. Susan Goldberg and Michael Lewis, "Play Behavior in the Year-Old Infant: Early Sex Differences," *Child Development,* 40 (1969), 21-30.

10. Jerome Kagan and Michael Lewis, "Studies of Attention in the Human Infant," *Merrill-Palmer Quarterly,* 2 (1965), 95-127.

11. Goldberg and Lewis, "Play Behavior in the Year-Old Infant," p. 29.

12. Meyer L. Rabban, "Sex Role Identification in Young Children in Two Diverse Social Groups," *Genetic Psychological Monographs,* 42 (1950), 81-158.

13. Evelyn Wiltshire Goodenough, "Interests in Persons as an Aspect of Sex Differences in the Early Years," *Genetic Psychological Monographs,* 55 (1957), 312.

14. Eleanor Maccoby and Carol Jacklin, *The Psychology of Sex Differences* (Stanford, Calif.: Stanford University Press, 1974).

15. Jeanne H. Block, "Another Look at Sex Differentiation in the Socialization Behaviors of Mothers and Fathers," in *Psychology of Women: Future Directions of Research.* (New York: Psychological Dimensions, 1978), forthcoming.

16. *Ibid.*

17. Aletha Huston-Stein and Ann Higgins-Trenk, "Development of Females from Childhood through Adulthood: Careers and Feminine Role Orientations," in Paul Baltes, ed., *Life-Span: Development and Behavior* (New York: Academic Press, 1978), p. 282, citing E. Mavis Hetherington, "The Effects of Familial Variables on Sex Typing, On Parent-Child Similarity, and on Imitation in Children," in J. P. Hill, ed., *Minnesota Symposia on Child Psychology,* vol 1 (Minneapolis: Univ of Minn Press, 1967).

18. Esther Blank Greif, "Sex Differences in Parent-Child Conversations: Who Interrupts Whom," paper presented at the meetings of the Society for Research on Child Development, San Francisco, March 1979.

19. Lenore J. Weitzman, Deborah Eifler, Elizabeth Hokada, and Catherine Ross, "Sex Role Socialization in Picture Books for Pre-School Children," *American Journal of Sociology,* May 1972.

20. *Ibid.,* p. 1128

21. *Ibid.,* p. 1129-30

22. *Ibid.,* p. 1140
23. *Ibid.,* p. 1141.
24. *Ibid.,* p. 1141.
25. *Ibid.* Parts of this quote were paraphrased from the original.
26. Jo Ann Gardner, "*Sesame Street* and Sex Role Stereotypes," in *Women,* 1, 3 (Spring 1970).
27. Sarah H. Sternglanz and Lisa A. Serbin, "Sex Role Stereotyping in Children's Television Programs," *Developmental Psychology,* 10, 5 (1974), 710-15.
28. *Ibid.*
29. *Ibid.,* p. 711.
30. *Ibid.,* p. 714.
31. Ruth E. Hartley, "Sex-Role Pressures and the Socialization of the Male Child," *Psychological Reports,* 5 (1959), 457-68, 461.
32. *Ibid.*
33. *Ibid.*
34. *Ibid.*
35. Rabban, "Sex Role Identification in Young Children," p. 145.
36. M. S. Simpson, "Parent Preferences of Young Children," *Contributing Education,* No. 682 (New York: Teachers College, Columbia University, 1935).
37. Daniel G. Brown, "Sex-Role Preference in Young Children," *Psychological Monographs,* 70, 14 (1956), 1-19.
38. *Ibid.*
39. Willard W. Hartup and Elsie A. Zook, "Sex-Role Preferences in Three- and Four-Year-Old Children," *Journal of Consulting Psychology,* 24 (December 1960), 420-26.
40. Willard W. Hartup, "Some Correlates of Parental Imitation in Young Children," *Child Development,* 33 (1962), 85-96.
41. Hartley, "Sex-Role Pressures."
42. *Ibid.*
43. Brown, "Sex-Role Preference in Young Children."
44. S. Smith, "Age and Sex Differences in Children's Opinion Concerning Sex Differences," *Journal of Genetic Psychology,* 54 (1939), 17-25.
45. *Ibid.*
46. David B. Lynn, *Parental and Sex Role Identification: A Theoretical Formulation* (Berkeley, Calif.: McCutchan Publishing, 1969), p. 24.
47. *Ibid.*
48. David B. Lynn, "A Note on Sex Differences in the Development of Masculine and Feminine Identification," *Psychological Review,* 66, 2 (1959), 126-35.
49. Hartley, "Sex-Role Pressures," p. 458.
50. *Ibid.*
51. For an excellent review of the learning literatures and the effects of punishment versus rewards, see William J. Goode, "The Uses of Dispraise," in *The Celebration of Heroes* (Berkeley, Calif.: University of California Press, 1978).
52. Hartley, "Sex-Role Pressures."

53. Ruth E. Hartley, "A Developmental View of Female Sex-Role Definition and Identification," *Merrill-Palmer Quarterly,* 10, 1 (January 1964), 3-17, 4.

54. Janet Lever, "Christmas Toys for Girls and Boys," report to Sociology 62a, Sociological Perspectives on Women, Sociology Department, Fall 1970, Yale University, Professor L. Weitzman.

55. William D. Ward, "Variance of Sex-Role Preference Among Boys and Girls," *Psychological Reports,* 23, 2 (1968), 467-70.

56. Komarovsky, *Women in the Modern World.*

57. *Ibid.*

58. Pauline R. Sears, Eleanor Maccoby, and Harry Levin, *Patterns of Child Rearing* (Evanston, Ill.: Row, Peterson, 1957).

59. Urie Bronfenbrenner, "Some Familial Antecedents of Responsibility and Leadership in Adolescents," in Luigi Petrullo and Bernard M. Bass, eds., *Leadership and Interpersonal Behavior* (New York: Holt, Rinehart, 1961).

60. Komarovsky, *Women in the Modern World,* p. 55.

61. Jerome Kagan, "Acquisition and Significance of Sex Typing and Sex-Role Identity," in Martin Leon Hoffman and Lois Wladis Hoffman, eds., *Review of Child Development Research* (New York: Russell Sage Foundation, 1964), pp. 137-67, 151.

62. Again, it is important to point out that these assertions about parental behavior are considered controversial and have not yet been "proven" in observational studies.

63. David Aberle and Kasper Naegele, "Middle Class Father's Occupational Role and Attitudes Toward Children," in Norman W. Bell and Ezra F. Vogel, eds., *The Family,* rev. ed. (New York: Free Press, 1968); Melvin L. Kohn, "Social Class and Parental Values," *American Journal of Sociology,* 64 (January 1959), 337-51; Sears, Maccoby, and Levin, *Patterns of Child Rearing;* and Paul H. Mussen, John U. Conger, and Jerome Kagan, *Child Development and Personality,* 2nd ed. (New York: Harper and Row, 1963).

64. Judith M. Bardwick, Elizabeth Douvan, Matina S. Horner, and David Gutmann, *Feminine Personality and Conflict* (Belmont, Calif.: Brooks/Cole, 1970), p. 4.

65. *Ibid.*

66. *Ibid.*

67. Kagan, "Acquisition and Significance of Sex Typing," p. 151.

68. *Ibid.*

69. Urie Bronfenbrenner, "The Changing American Child: A Speculative Analysis," *Merrill-Palmer Quarterly,* 7 (April 1961), 9, 73-83.

70. Stanley Schachter, *The Psychology of Affiliation* (Stanford, Calif.: Stanford University Press, 1959); Bronfenbrenner, "The Changing American Child."

71. Bronfenbrenner, "The Changing American Child."

72. Of course these speculations are considered controversial and have not been "proven." They should provide an interesting and challenging arena for future research.

73. Kagan, "Acquisition and Significance of Sex Typing," p. 151.

74. Personal conversation, December 1971.

75. Lisa A. Serbin, K. Daniel O'Leary, Ronald N. Kent, and Ilene J. Tolnick, "A

Comparison of Teacher Response to the Preacademic and Problem Behavior of Boys and Girls," *Child Development,* 44, 4 (December 1973), 776-804.

76.　K. D. O'Leary, K. Kaufman, R. Kass, and R. Drabman, "The Effects of Loud and Soft Reprimands on Behavior of Disruptive Students," *Exceptional Children,* 37 (1970), 145-55, as cited in Serbin *et al.,* "Comparison of Teacher Response," p. 797.

77.　E. M. Pinkston, N. M. Reese, J. M. LeBlanc, and D. M. Baer, "Independent Control of Aggression and Peer Interaction by Contingent Teacher Attention," *Journal of Applied Behavior Analysis,* in press, as cited in Serbin *et al.,* "Comparison of Teacher Response," p. 797.

78.　Serbin *et al.,* "Comparison of Teacher Response," p. 797.

79.　*Ibid.,* p. 800.

80.　*Ibid.,* p. 800.

81.　*Ibid.,* p. 801.

82.　*Ibid.,* p. 802.

83.　*Ibid.,* p. 802.

84.　*Ibid.,* p. 802.

85.　Carol Nagy Jacklin, "Sex Differences and Their Relationship to Sex Equity in Learning and Teaching," paper prepared for the National Institute of Education, September 1977, p. 3.

86.　D. R. Omark, M. Omark, and M. Edelman, "Dominance Hierarchies in Young Children," paper presented at International Congress of Anthropological and Ethnological Sciences, Chicago, 1973.

87.　D. A. Parton and Y. Geshuri, "Learning of Aggression as a Function of Presence of a Human Model, Response Intensity, and Target of the Response," *Journal of Experimental Child Psychology,* 11 (1971), 491-504.

88.　R. G. Slaby, "Verbal Regulation of Aggression and Altruism in Children," paper presented at the First International Conference of the "Determinants and Origins of Aggressive Behavior," Monte Carlo, 1973.

89.　J. R. Shortell and H. B. Biller, "Aggression in Children as a Function of Sex of Object and Sex of Opponent," *Developmental Psychology,* 3 (1970), 143-44 (brief report).

90.　Jacklin, "Sex Differences," p. 3.

91.　*Ibid.,* p. 3.

92.　*Ibid.,* p. 3.

93.　*Ibid.,* p. 3.

NOTES TO CHAPTER 2

1.　Leona E. Tyler, "Sex Differences" under "Individual Differences" in the *International Encyclopedia of the Social Sciences,* vol. 7 (New York: Macmillan, 1968), pp. 207-13.

2.　Jo Freeman, "The Social Construction of the Second Sex," in Michele Barskof, ed., *Roles Women Play* (Belmont, Calif.: Brooks/Cole, 1971), p. 127.

3.　See, for example, Leona E. Tyler, *The Psychology of Human Differences* (New York: Appleton-Century-Crofts, 1965).

91

4. Eleanor Maccoby and Carol Jacklin, *The Psychology of Sex Differences* (Stanford, Calif.: Stanford University Press, 1974).

5. *Ibid.,* p. 349.

6. See for example Jeanne H. Block, "Issues, Problems and Pitfalls in Assessing Sex Differences: A Critical Review of the Psychology of Sex Differences," *Merrill-Palmer Quarterly,* 22, 4 (1976), 308.

7. For a more extensive review of the literature, see William J. Goode, Elizabeth Hopkins, and Helen M. McClure, *Social Systems and Family Structures* (Indianapolis: Bobbs-Merrill, 1971).

8. Letha Scanzoni and John Scanzoni, *Men, Women and Change: A Sociology of Marriage and Family* (New York: McGraw-Hill, 1976), p. 30.

9. Goode *et al., Social Systems and Family Structures.*

10. Meyer L. Rabban, "Sex Role Identification in Young Children in Two Diverse Social Groups," *Genetic Psychological Monographs,* 42 (1950), 81-158.

11. *Ibid.*

12. *Ibid.*

13. Scanzoni and Scanzoni, *Men, Women and Change,* p. 35.

14. Lillian Rubin, *Worlds of Pain: Life in the Working Class Family* (New York: Basic Books, 1976), pp. 125-26.

15. See, for example, Herbert Gans, *The Urban Villagers* (New York: Free Press, 1962).

16. Although there has been no systematic study of racial differences in parental treat-ment of young children, we do know that black mothers, irrespective of class, have much less exposure to child-rearing experts. See, for example, Zena Smith Blau, "Exposure to Child-Rearing Experts: A Structural Interpretation of Class-Color Differences," *American Journal of Sociology,* 69 (May 1964), 596-608.

17. Fred Strodbeck, "Family Interaction, Values, and Achievement," in David McClelland, Alfred Baldwin, Urie Bronfenbrenner, and Fred Strodbeck, eds., *Talent and Society* (Princeton, N.J.: Van Nostrand, 1968), pp. 135-94.

18. Personal conversation, Winter 1971.

19. I am indebted to Marjorie Randon Hershey of the Department of Political Science at Indiana University for her helpful suggestions in a personal conversation in April 1978.

20. Arlie R. Hochschild, "A Review of Sex Role Research," *American Journal of Sociology,* 78 (1973), 1011, 1023.

21. Joyce Aschenbrenner, *Lifelines: Black Families in Chicago* (New York: Holt, Rine-hart and Winston, 1975), p. 6.

22. Denise Kandel, "Race, Maternal Authority, and Adolescent Aspiration," *American Journal of Sociology,* 76 (1971), 999-1020.

23. Daniel P. Moynihan, *The Negro Family: The Case for National Action* (Washington, D.C.: U.S. Department of Labor, Office of Policy Planning and Research, 1965).

24. Carol B. Stack, *All Our Kin: Strategies for Survival in a Black Community* (New York: Harper Colophon Books, 1974), p. 121.

25. *Ibid.,* pp. 122-26.

26. *Ibid.*

27. *Ibid.,* p. 112.

28. *Ibid.,* p. 113.

29. Marjorie Randon Hershey, "Racial Differences in Sex Role Identities and Sex Role Stereotyping," *Social Science Quarterly* (1978). See also B. F. Turner and C. B. Turner, "The Political Implications of Social Stereotyping of Women and Men among Black and White College Students," *Sociology and Social Research,* 58 (1974), 155-62.

30. Joyce A. Ladner, *Tomorrow's Tomorrow: The Black Woman* (Garden City, N.Y.: Doubleday, 1971), pp. 187-88.

31. Tansey Thomas, "Growing Up in the Ghetto," student report, Sociology 131, University of California, Davis, Fall 1971.

32. Ladner, *Tomorrow's Tomorrow,* pp. 120-76.

33. Jo Freeman, personal conversation, April 1978.

34. Cynthia Epstein, "Positive Effects of the Multiple Negative: Explaining the Success of Black Professional Women," *American Journal of Sociology,* 78 (1973), 913-18.

35. Kandel, "Race, Maternal Authority, and Adolescent Aspiration," p. 1009.

36. Ladner, *Tomorrow's Tomorrow,* pp. 120-76.

37. *Ibid.*

38. *Ibid.,* pp. 187-88.

39. Patricia Gurin and Carolyn Gaylord, "Educational and Occupational Goals of Men and Women at Black Colleges," *Monthly Labor Review,* June 1976, p. 10.

40. *Ibid.*

41. Hershey, "Racial Differences in Sex Role Identities."

42. *Ibid.,* p. 12.

43. Hershey, personal conversation, April 1978.

44. *Ibid.*

45. John H. Scanzoni, *The Black Family in Modern Society,* Phoenix Edition (Chicago: University of Chicago Press, 1977), p. 335.

46. See, for example, Sandra L. Bem, "Beyond Androgyny: Some Presumptuous Prescriptions for a Liberated Sexual Identity," in J. Sherman and F. Denmark, eds., *Psychology of Women: Future Directions of Research* (New York: Psychological Dimensions, 1976).

47. Orville G. Brim, "Family Structure and Sex Role Learning by Children," *Sociometry,* 21 (1958), 1-16; Helen L. Koch, "The Relation of Certain Family Constellation Characteristics and the Attitudes of Children Towards Adults," *Child Development,* 26 (March 1955), 13-40.

48. Janet G. Hunt and Larry L. Hunt, "Race, Daughters and Father-Loss: Does Absence Make the Girl Grow Stronger?", *Social Problems,* 25, 1 (1977), 91.

NOTES TO CHAPTER 3

1. Ruth E. Hartley, "A Developmental View of Female Sex-Role Definition and Identification," *Merrill-Palmer Quarterly,* 10, 1 (January 1964), 3-17, 4.

2. Irwin Child, Elmer Potter, and Estelle Levine, "Children's Textbooks and Personality Development: An Exploration in the Social Psychology of Education," in Morris L. Haimowitz and Natalie Reader Haimowitz, eds., *Human Development: Selected Readings* (New York: Thomas Y. Crowell, 1960), pp. 292-305.

3. *Ibid.*, p. 302.

4. Women on Words and Images, *Dick and Jane as Victims* (Princeton, N.J., 1972); Marcia Federbush, *"Let Them Aspire"* (Ann Arbor, Mich., 1972); and Terry Sario, Carol Nagy Jacklin, and Carol Kehr Tittle, "Sex Role Stereotyping in the Public Schools," *Harvard Educational Review,* 43, 3 (August 1973), 386-404.

5. Lenore J. Weitzman and Diane Rizzo, *Images of Males and Females in Elementary School Textbooks* (New York: National Organization for Women's Legal Defense and Education Fund, 1974).

6. *Ibid.*

7. Saario, Jacklin, and Tittle, "Sex Role Stereotyping in the Public Schools."

8. *Ibid.*, p. 404.

9. *Ibid.*

10. *Ibid.*, pp. 406-07.

11. Project on Equal Educational Rights, "Stalled at the Start: Government Action on Sex Bias in the Schools" (Washington, D.C., 1978), p. 13.

12. *Ibid.*, p. 7

13. *Ibid.*, p. 7, 13, 21.

14. Lisa A. Serbin, K. Daniel O'Leary, Ronald N. Kent, and Ilene J. Tolnick, "A Comparison of Teacher Response to the Preacademic and Problem Behavior of Boys and Girls," *Child Development,* 44, 4 (December 1973), 776-804.

15. W. J. Meyer and G. C. Thompson, "Sex Differences in the Distribution of Teacher Approval among Sixth Grade Children," *Journal of Educational Psychology,* 47 (1956), 385-96.

16. See, generally, Carol S. Dweck and Ellen S. Bush, "Sex Differences in Learned Helplessness: I. Differential Debilitation with Peer and Adult Evaluators," *Developmental Psychology,* 12, 2 (1976), 147-56; and Carol S. Dweck, William Davidson, Sharon Nelson, and Bradley Enna, "Sex Differences in Learned Helplessness: II. The Contingencies of Evaluative Feedback in the Classroom and III. An Experimental Analysis," *Developmental Psychology,* 14, 3 (1978), 268-76.

17. Carol S. Dweck and N. D. Reppucci, "Learned Helplessness and Reinforcement Responsibility in Children," *Journal of Personality and Social Psychology,* 25 (1973), 109-16.

18. *Ibid.*

19. Dweck *et al.,* "Sex Differences . . . II," p. 269.

20. *Ibid.*

21. *Ibid.*

22. *Ibid.*, p. 270.

23. *Ibid.*, p. 271-72.

24. *Ibid.*, p. 274.

25. Eleanor E. Maccoby, "Sex Differences in Intellectual Functioning," in E. E. Maccoby, ed., *The Development of Sex Differences* (Stanford, Calif.: Stanford University Press, 1966).

26. G. A. Milton, *Five Studies of the Relation Between Sex Role Identification and Achievement in Problem Solving,* Technical Report No. 3, Dept. of Industrial Administration, Department of Psychology, Yale University, December 1958.

27. *Ibid.*

28. Jerome Kagan, "Acquisition and Significance of Sex Typing and Sex-Role Identity," in Martin Leon Hoffman and Lois Wladis Hoffman, eds., *Review of Child Development Research* (New York: Russell Sage Foundation, 1964), pp. 137-67, 157.

29. Eleanor E. Maccoby, "Woman's Intellect," in Seymour L. Farber and Roger H. L. Wilson, eds., *The Potential of Women,* (New York: McGraw-Hill, 1963), p. 31.

30. Julia A. Sherman, "Problems of Sex Differences in Space Perception and Aspects of Intellectual Function," *Psychological Review,* 74, 4 (1967), 290-99.

31. *Ibid.*

32. *Ibid.*

33. The following is paraphrased from comments of Professor William Goode, Jo Freeman, and myself in personal communications, 1971-72.

34. Similar assumptions about the linkage of male abilities and the traits most useful in managerial positions have been challenged in William J. Goode, "Family Life of the Successful Woman," in Eli Ginzberg and Alice Yohalem, eds., *Corporate Lib* (Baltimore: Johns Hopkins University Press, 1973), pp. 97-117.

35. Elizabeth Fennema and Julia Sherman, "Sex-Related Differences in Mathematics Achievement: Spatial Visualization and Affective Factors," *American Educational Research Journal,* 14, 1 (Winter 1977), p. 66.

36. *Ibid.*

37. David Aberle and Kasper Naegele, "Middle Class Father's Occupational Role and Attitudes Toward Children," in Norman W. Bell and Ezra F. Vogel, eds., *The Family,* rev. ed. (New York: Free Press, 1968).

38. *Ibid.*

39. This finding is taken from Table 4, p. 569, in William H. Sewell and Vimal P. Shah, "Social Class, Parental Encouragement, and Educational Aspirations," *American Journal of Sociology,* 73, 5 (March 1968), 559-72.

40. David Bordua, "Educational Aspirations and Parental Stress on College," *Social Forces,* 38 (1960), 267.

41. Glen H. Elder, Jr., *Adolescent Achievement and Mobility Aspirations* (Chapel Hill, N.C.: Institute for Research in Social Science, 1962), pp. 159-60.

42. Sex differences in parental encouragement persist even when social class and intelligence are held constant; Sewell and Shah, "Social Class, Parental Encouragement, and Educational Aspirations," p. 570.

43. Joyce A. Ladner, *Tomorrow's Tomorrow: The Black Woman* (Garden City, N.Y.: Doubleday, 1971).

44. Denise Kandel, "Race, Maternal Authority, and Adolescent Aspiration," *American Journal of Sociology,* 76 (1971), 999-1020, p. 1009.

45. Mirra Komarovsky, "Functional Analysis of Sex Roles," *American Sociological Review,* 15 (August 1950), 508-16.
46. *Ibid.*
47. *Ibid.*
48. Kenneth Keniston and Ellen Keniston, "An American Anachronism: The Image of Women and Work," *The American Scholar,* 33, 3 (Summer 1964), 355-75.
49. James V. Pierce, "Sex Differences in Achievement Motivation of Able High School Students," Cooperative Research Project No. 1097, University of Chicago, December 1961.
50. *Ibid.*
51. Keniston and Keniston, "An American Anachronism."
52. I am indebted to Sheila Tobias, Associate Provost of Wesleyan University, for suggesting this term to me.
53. Lillian Rubin, *Worlds of Pain: Life in the Working Class Family* (New York: Basic Books, 1976), pp. 40-41.
54. *Ibid.*

NOTES TO CHAPTER 4

1. Mirra Komarovsky, "Cultural Contradictions and Sex Roles," *American Journal of Sociology,* 52 (1946), 184-89.
2. *Ibid.*
3. Personal conversation, January 1971.
4. Florence Howe, "Identity and Expression: A Writing Course for Women," unpublished paper.
5. Lois W. Hoffman, "The Employment of Women, Education and Fertility" in Martha Mednick, Sandra Tangri, and Lois Hoffman, eds., *Women and Achievement* (New York: John Wiley and Sons, 1975), pp. 110-14.
6. R. A. Van Dusen and Eleanor B. Sheldon, "The Changing Status of American Women: A Life Cycle Perspective," *American Psychologist,* 31 (1976), 106-16.
7. *Ibid.*
8. *Ibid.,* citing U.S. Department of Labor, *Manpower Report to the President* (Washington, D.C.: U.S. Government Printing Office, 1975).
9. Van Dusen and Sheldon, "The Changing Status of American Women."
10. J. L. McCarthy and D. Wolfle. "Doctorates Granted to Women and Minority Group Members," *Science,* 189 (1975), 856-59; and J. B. Parrish, "Women in Professional Training," *Monthly Labor Review,* 97 (May 1974), 40-43.
11. Van Dusen and Sheldon, "The Changing Status of American Women," citing U.S. Department of Labor, *Manpower Report to the President.*
12. Alice Rossi, "Equality Between the Sexes," in Robert J. Lifton, ed., *The Woman in America* (Boston: Houghton Mifflin, 1964).
13. Elizabeth Douvan, "Sex Differences in Adolescent Character Processes," *Merrill Palmer Quarterly,* 6 (1960), 203-11.

14. Patricia Cross, *Beyond the Open Door* (San Francisco: Jossey-Bass, 1971), p. 148.

15. Laurie Davidson Cummings, "Value Stretch in Definitions of Career Among College Women: Horatia Alger As Feminist Model," *Social Problems,* 25, 1 (1977), 65-74; and Ann P. Parelius, "Change and Stability in College Women's Orientations toward Education, Family and Work," *Social Problems,* 22 (February 1975), 420-32.

16. *Virginia Slims American Women's Opinion Poll,* III, n.d., p. 1; and "Women in America," *The Gallup Opinion Index,* Report 128 (March 1976), p. 30.

17. Matina S. Horner, "Women's Need to Fail," *Psychology Today,* (November 1969), pp. 36-38, 62.

18. *Ibid.,* p. 38.

19. *Ibid.*

20. *Ibid.*

21. Horner, "Women's Need to Fail;" and Matina S. Horner, "Toward an Understanding of Achievement-Related Conflicts in Women," *The Journal of Social Issues,* 28, 2 (1972), 157-75.

22. Mednick *et al., Women and Achievement,* p. 124.

23. Horner, "Women's Need to Fail," p. 62.

24. Carol Tavris and Carole Offir, *The Longest War: Sex Differences in Perspective* (New York: Harcourt Brace, 1977), p. 191.

25. David Tresemer, "Fear of Success: Popular, But Unproven," *Psychology Today,* 7 (March 1974), 82-85.

26. Lois Wladis Hoffman, "Fear of Success in Males and Females: 1965 and 1971," *Journal of Consulting and Clinical Psychology,* 42 (1974), 353-58.

27. Lillian Robbins and Edwin Robbins, comment on "Toward an Understanding of Achievement-related Conflicts in Women," *Journal of Social Issues,* 29, 1 (1973), 133-37, as cited in Tavris and Offir, *The Longest War.*

28. John Condry and Sharon Dyer, "Fear of Success: Attribution of Cause to the Victim," *Journal of Social Issues,* 32, 3 (1976), 63-83, as paraphrased in Tavris and Offir, *The Longest War,* p. 193.

29. Tavris and Offir, *The Longest War,* p. 193.

30. Tresemer, "Fear of Success."

31. See, for example, Cynthia Epstein, *Woman's Place: Options and Limits in Professional Careers* (Berkeley: University of California Press, 1970).

32. Hoffman, "The Employment of Women," p. 114.

33. L. W. Hoffman and M. L. Hoffman, "The Value of Children to Parents," in J. T. Fawcett, ed., *Psychological Perspectives on Population* (New York: Basic Books, 1973).

34. A. G. Levine, "Marital and Occupational Plans of Women in Professional Schools: Law, Medicine, Nursing, Teaching," Ph.D. dissertation, Yale University, 1968.

35. M. Komarovsky, "Cultural Contradictions and Sex Roles: The Masculine Case," *American Journal of Sociology,* 78, 4 (197℃,, 873-84.

36. Hoffman, "The Employment of Women," p. 115.

37. *Ibid.*

38. See, for example, J. A. Birnbaum, "Life Patterns, Personality Style and Self Esteem in Gifted Family Oriented and Career-Committed Women," Ph.D. dissertation, University of Michigan, 1971; Lynda Lytle Holmstrom, *The Two-Career Family* (Cambridge, Mass.: Schenckman, 1972); and T. N. Garland, "The Better Half? The Male in the Dual Profession Family," in C. Safilios-Rothschild, ed., *Toward a Sociology of Women* (Lexington, Mass.: Xerox College Publishing, 1972).

39. Aletha Huston-Stein and Ann Higgins-Trenk, "Development of Females from Childhood through Adulthood: Careers and Feminine Role Orientations," in Paul B. Baltes, ed., *Life-Span Development and Behavior* (New York: Academic Press, 1978), p. 268.

40. Komarovsky, "Cultural Contradictions and Sex Roles: The Masculine Case."

41. Huston-Stein and Higgins-Trenk "Development of Females," p. 268.

42. *Ibid.,* p. 267, citing E. M. Almquist, "Sex Stereotypes in Occupational Choice: The Case for College Women," *Journal of Vocational Behavior,* 5 (1974), 13-21.

43. Komarovsky, "Cultural Contradictions and Sex Roles: The Masculine Case."

44. Cummings, "Value Stretch in Definitions of Career."

45. *Ibid.,* p. 72.

46. Van Dusen and Sheldon, "The Changing Status of American Women," p. 175.

47. *Ibid.,* p. 179.

48. Huston-Stein and Higgins-Trenk, "Development of Females," p. 278.

49. Van Dusen and Sheldon, "The Changing Status of American Women," p. 180.

50. *Ibid.,* p. 179.

NOTES TO CHAPTER 5

1. Lucy Sells, "Mathematics—A Critical Filter," *The Science Teacher,* February 1978, pp. 28-29.

2. John Ernest, "Mathematics and Sex," April 1976 (preprint of an article to appear in the *American Mathematical Monthly*), p. 6.

3. Elizabeth Fennema, "Mathematics Learning and the Sexes: A Review," *Journal for Research in Mathematics Education,* 5 (1974), 126-39.

4. Ernest, "Mathematics and Sex," p. 3.

5. *Ibid.,* p. 4.

6. *Ibid.*

7. *Ibid.,* p. 5.

8. Lynn H. Fox, "Facilitating the Development of Mathematical Talent in Young Women," Ph.D. dissertation, John Hopkins University, 1974.

9. "Math Mystique: Fear of Figuring," *Time,* March 14, 1977, p. 36.

10. Sanford Dornbusch, "To Try or Not to Try," *Stanford Magazine,* 2, 2 (1974), 50-54.

11. *Ibid.*

12. Elizabeth Fennema and Julia A. Sherman, "Sexual Stereotyping and Mathematics Learning," to appear in *The Arithmetic Teacher.*

13. Sheila Tobias, *Overcoming Math Anxiety* (New York: W. W. Norton, 1978), Chapter 3, "Mathematics and Sex."

14. Lenore J. Weitzman and Diane Rizzo, "Sex Role Stereotypes in Elementary School Textbooks in Five Subject Areas," in *Biased Textbooks* (Washington, D.C.: National Education Association, 1974).

15. Ernest, "Mathematics and Sex," p. 6.

16. Dornbusch, "To Try or Not to Try."

17. Sheila Tobias, "Math Anxiety: Why Is a Smart Girl Like You Counting on Your Fingers?", *Ms Magazine*. See also Tobias, *Overcoming Math Anxiety*, especially Chapter 3.

18. Tobias, "Math Anxiety," p. 57.

19. Lynn H. Fox, "Sex Differences in Mathematical Precocity: Bridging the Gap," in Daniel P. Keating, ed., *Intellectual Talent: Research and Development*, Proceedings of the Sixth Annual Hyman Blumberg Symposium on Research in Early Childhood Education (Baltimore: The Johns Hopkins University Press, 1970).

20. *Ibid.*, p. 187.

21. *Ibid.*, p. 188.

22. *Ibid.*, p. 189.

23. *Ibid.*, p. 203.

24. *Ibid.*, p. 204.

25. *Ibid.*, p. 209.

26. *Ibid.*, p. 204.

27. Quoted in Ernest, "Mathematics and Sex," p. 12.

28. Tobias, *Overcoming Math Anxiety*, Chapter 3.

NOTES TO CHAPTER 6

1. Aletha Huston-Stein and Ann Higgins-Trenk, "Development of Females from Childhood Through Adulthood: Careers and Feminine Role Orientations," in Paul B. Baltes, ed., *Life-Span Development and Behavior* (New York: Academic Press, 1978), pp. 279-80.

2. Ruth E. Hartley, "Children's Concept of Male and Female Roles," *Merrill-Palmer Quarterly*, 6 (1960), 83-91.

3. *Ibid.*

4. Huston-Stein and Higgins-Trenk, "Development of Females," citations omitted, pp. 279-80. While daughters of employed mothers did not differ in career aspirations in two of the studies cited, they did have more favorable attitudes about careers for women.

5. *Ibid.*, citations omitted.

6. *Ibid.*, p. 281.

7. Paul H. Mussen, "Early Sex-Role Development," in David A. Goslin, ed., *Handbook of Socialization Theory and Research* (Chicago: Rand McNally, 1969).

8. *Ibid.*

9. Talcott Parsons, "Family Structure and the Socialization of the Child," in Talcott

Parsons and Robert F. Bales, eds., *Family, Socialization, and Interaction Process* (New York: Free Press, 1955), p. 80.

10. Philip Slater, "Parental Role Differentiation," *The American Journal of Sociology*, 47, 3 (November 1961), 296-331.

11. William J. Goode, personal conversation, December 1970.

12. David McClelland, *The Achieving Society* (New York: Free Press, 1964).

13. Alfred B. Heilbrun, Jr., "Sex Role, Instrumental-Expressive Behavior, and Psychopathology in Females," *Journal of Abnormal Psychology*, 73, 2 (1958), 131-36.

14. Huston-Stein and Higgins-Trenk, "Development of Females," p. 282.

15. Mussen, "Early Sex-Role Development"; and Walter Mischel, "A Social-Learning View of Sex Differences," in Eleanor E. Maccoby, ed., *The Development of Sex Differences* (Stanford, Calif.: Stanford University Press, 1966).

16. Sheila Tobias, personal conversation, April 1978.

17. Nancy Potter, "Mathematical and Verbal Ability Patterns in Women," Ph.D. dissertation, University of Missouri-Columbia, 1974.

18. Heilbrun, "Sex Role . . . in Females," p. 134.

19. Abraham H. Maslow, "Dominance, Personality and Social Behavior in Women," *Journal of Social Psychology*, 10 (1942), 259-94.

20. Jessie Bernard, "The Myth of the Happy Marriage," in V. Gornick and R. Morgan, eds., *Women in a Sexist Society* (New York: Basic Books, 1971); and *The Future of Marriage* (New York: World Books, 1972).

21. Betty Friedan, *The Feminine Mystique* (New York: W. W. Norton, 1963).

22. Roxann A. Van Dusen and Eleanor Bernert Sheldon, "The Changing Status of American Women: A Life Cycle Perspective," *The American Psychologist*, 31 (February 1976), pp. 106-16.

23. *Ibid.* The enrollment of men between 25 and 34 also increased between 1970 and 1974—by 46 percent.

24. *Ibid.*

25. *Ibid.*

26. Huston-Stein and Higgins-Trenk, "Development of Females."

27. Orville G. Brim, Jr., "Theories of the Male Mid-Life Crises," *Counseling Psychologist: Counseling Adults* (1976), Special Issue.

28. Saul D. Feldman, "Impediment or Stimulant? Marital Status and Graduate Education" in J. Huber, ed., *Changing Women in a Changing Society* (Chicago: University of Chicago Press, 1973), p. 231.

29. James V. Pierce, "Sex Differences in Achievement Motivation of Able High School Students," Cooperative Research Project No. 1097, University of Chicago, December 1961.

30. Tobias, personal conversation, April 1978.

31. Jean M. Press and Fraine E. Whitney, "Achievement Syndromes in Women: Vicarious or Conflict-Ridden," paper presented at the Forty-first Annual Meeting of the Eastern Sociological Society, April 1971; and Jean Lippman-Blumen, "How Ideology Shapes Women's Lives," *Scientific American*, 226, 1 (January 1972).

32. Press and Whitney, "Achievement Syndromes in Women."

Index

Aberle, D., 43, 44, 90, 95

Achievement: motivation, 28, 34, 79, 85; test, 36-37; vicarious, 85-86; by women, 49, 75-86

Adolescence, 14, 69

Aggression, 3, 18, 20, 21; verbal, 22

All in the Family, 26

Almquist, E. M., 98

Analytical ability, 41-43

Anxiety, 14, 15, 17, 19, 59, 60, 61

Apgar score, 2

Approval, 18

Aschenbrenner, 5, 92

Assertion, 21n

Athletics, 38, 70

Attractiveness, 46

Baer, D. M., 91

Bardwick, J. M., 18, 90

Behavior: dependent, 19, 20, 82; differences. 3, 21-22, 23-34; disruptive, 19, 20, 21, 39; dominance, 22, 51; expressive, 26, 27

Bem, D., x

Bem, S. L., x, 33, 93

Bernard, J., 82, 100

Biller, H. B., 21, 91

Birman, J., 73, 74

Birnbaum, J. A., 98

Black woman, 28-34, 44, 81
Blau, Z. S., 92
Block, J. H., 5, 88, 92
Book: picture, 6-9, 10, 83; text-, 36, 70, 83
Bordua, D., 44, 95
Brim, O. G., 34, 92, 100
Bronfenbrenner, U., 18, 90
Brown, D. G., 12, 89
Bunting, P., 55
Bush, E. S., 39, 94
Business, 56

Caldecott Medal, 7-8
Career, 44, 63; continuous, 63, 64; vs. job, 57, 64; vs. marriage, 56, 58
Child, I., 36, 94
Children, 64, 65
Class, 44, 47
College, 44, 48-66
Competition, 59-60, 72
Condry, J., 60, 97
Cooperative activity, 72
Cross, P., 58, 97
Cross-cultural study, 5, 21
Cross-sex preference, 12
Cuddliness, 2
Cummings, L. D., 58, 63, 64, 66

Datan, N., 2, 88
Davidson, W., 39, 94
Dependency, 19, 20, 82
Differential treatment, 2-4
Discrimination: in athletics, 38; occupational, 86
Disruptive behavior, 19, 20, 21, 39
Doctoral degree, 56-57
Doll play, 19
Dominance, 22, 51
Dornbusch, S., 69, 70, 98, 99
Douvan, E., 57, 90, 96
Drabman, R., 20, 91
Dweck, C. S., 39, 40, 94
Dyer, S., 60, 97

Edelman, M., 21, 91
Education, 83; aspirations for, 31, 45; continuing, 84; professional, 30, 56-57
Edwards, C. P., xi
Egalitarian marriage, 64

Ehrhardt, A. A., xi, 87
Eifler, D., 7, 88
Elder, G. H. Jr., 44, 95
Encouragement, 55, 56; by father, 79; lack of, 71n
Engineering, 56
Enna, B., 39, 94
Epstein, C., 30, 93, 97
Ernest, J., 68, 69, 70-71, 98, 99
Ethnicity, 27-28
Evaluative feedback, 40, 41
Expectation: class-related, 26-27; and intellectual achievement, 54-58; sex-related, 10-11, 43

Faculty, 54
Failure, 39, 40, 41
Family, 25, 29, 30, 34; of achiever, 76-80
Father: absence, 14, 34; and femininity, 78-79; and homework, 69; interruption by, 6; as model, 13; occupational status of, 80; and sex typing, 5
Fear of success, 59-61, 83
Feldman, S. D., 85, 100
Federbush, M., 94
Femininity, 15, 17, 19, 33, 59-61, 62, 78-79; loss of, 42, 45, 59
Feminist behavior study, 50-54
Fennema, E., 43, 70, 95, 98
Fox, L. H., 69, 72, 73, 98, 99
Freeman, J., 24, 91, 93, 95
Freud, S., 12n
Freudian theory, 5, 12n, 78
Friedan, B., 82
Fulfillment, 82

Gans, H., 92
Gardner, J. A., 9, 89
Garland, T. N., 98
Gaylord, C., 31, 32, 93
Geshuri, Y., 21, 91
Ghetto, 30, 31
Goal directedness, 82
Goldberg, S., 3, 88
Goode, W. J., 79, 89, 92, 95, 100
Goodenough, E. W., 5, 88
Graduate school, 56-57, 63
Gurin, P., 31, 32

Gutmann, D., 90

Hampson, J., xi, 87
Hampson, J. L., xi, 87
Hartley, R. E., 10, 11, 12, 14, 89, 90, 93, 99
Hartup, W. W., 12, 89
Heilbrun, A. B., 80, 82, 100
Hermaphrodite, xi
Hershey, M. R., 32, 33, 92, 93
Herzog, E., x
Hetherington, E. M., 88
Higgins-Trenk, A., 55, 63, 65n, 77, 78, 84, 88, 98, 99, 100
Hochschild, A., 92
Hoffman, L. W., 60n, 62, 96, 97
Hoffman, M. L., 97
Hokada, E., 7
Holmstrom, L. L., 98
Hopkins, E., 92
Horner, M. S., 28, 53, 59, 61, 90, 97
Howe, F., 55, 96
Hunt, J. G., 34, 93
Hunt, L. L., 34, 93
Huston-Stein, A., 55, 63, 65n, 77, 78, 84, 88, 98, 99, 100

Identification, 4-5; theory, 78
Identity, 57
Imitation, 10
Independence, 18, 33, 42
Individual differences, 23-24
Intellectual ability, 41-43, 53, 54-58
Interpersonal sensitivity, 82
Interruption, 6

Jacklin, C. N., 6, 21, 22, 25, 38, 91, 92, 94

Kagan, J., 18, 19, 88, 90, 95
Kandel, D., 29, 44, 92, 93, 95
Kass, R., 20, 91
Kaufman, K., 20, 91
Keniston, E., 45, 96
Keniston, K., 45, 96
Kent, R. N., 90, 94
Komarovsky, M., 16, 45, 49, 63, 88, 90, 96, 97, 98

Ladner, J. A., 30, 31, 32, 33, 93, 95

Language, 43
Law, 56, 62, 77
Learned difference, xi
Learned helplessness, 39, 40
Learning, 13-19
LeBlanc, J. M., 91
Lever, J., 90
Levin, H., 90
Levine, A. G., 97
Levine, E., 36, 94
Lewis, M., 3, 88
Lipman-Blumen, J., 85, 100
Lloyd, P. C., x
Luria, Z., 1, 2
Lynn, D. B., 13

Maccoby, E., 6, 25, 90, 92, 95
Marriage: age at, 64; vs. career, 56, 58; dual career, 63; egalitarian, 64
Masculinity, 33, 62
Maslow, A., 100
Mass media, 46
Maternal contact, 3
Math anxiety, 71, 74n
Mathematics, 41-43, 66-74; as male domain, 70, 71
Matriarch, 29
Matza, D., 19
McCarthy, J. L., 96
McClelland, D., 79, 100
McClure, H. M., 92
Mead, M., ix, 87
Medicine, 56, 62, 77
Mednick, M., 60n
Meyer, W. J., 39, 94
Midlife crisis, 84-85
Milton, G. A., 41, 95
Modeling, 5, 10, 13, 17, 29, 78
Money, J., xi, 87
Moss, H. A., 3, 88
Mother: employment of, 77, 78; and homework, 69; as model, 13, 29, 78; preference for, 12; role of, 8, 62
Movies, 83
Moynihan, D. P., 29, 92
Mussen, P. H., 99, 100

Naegele, K., 43, 44, 90, 95

Nelson, S., 39, 94
Newborn infant, 1-2
Nonexpectations, 54-58
Nurturance, 18, 26, 33, 78

Occupational aspiration, 63
Oedipal effect, 2
Offir, C., 60, 88, 97
O'Leary, K. D., 20, 90, 91, 94
Omark, D. R., 21, 91
Omark, M., 21, 91
Oversocialization, 80-85

Parelius, A. P., 58, 97
Parent: contact, 13; influence of, 43-45, 69, 83
Parsons, T., 100
Parton, D. A., 21, 91
Passivity, 18, 82
Peer: counseling, 74n; influence, 45-46, 49-54, 69, 83
Physical punishment, 17, 18
Pierce, J. V., 46, 85, 96, 100
Pinkston, D. A., 91
Potter, E., 36, 82, 94, 100
Preference: for math, 68-69; for parent, 4, 11-13
Premarital pregnancy, 29
Press, J. M., 85, 100, 101
Prestige, 12, 13, 62, 76
Professional education, 30, 56-57
Professional position, 30-31, 37, 44, 57, 62, 76, 77
Provenzano, F. J., 1, 2, 88
Psychological punishment, 18
Punishment, 14, 16, 17-19

Rabban, M. L., 4, 12, 88, 89, 92
Race, 28-34
Reentry woman, 84-85
Reese, N. M., 91
Rejection, 18
Reppucci, N. D., 94
Research: cross-cultural, 5, 21; needed, 29
Reward, 79; vs. punishment, 14, 17-19
Rizzo, D., 36, 70, 94, 99
Robbins, E., 97
Robbins, L., 97

Rosaldo, M. Z., x, 87
Ross, C., 7, 88
Rossi, A., 13n, 57, 96
Rubin, L., 1, 2, 27, 47, 96
Russell, B., 43

Scanzoni, J. H., 26, 33, 92, 93
Scanzoni, L., 26, 92
Schachter, S., 90
School, 36-43, 46-67
Sears, P. R., 90
Self, P., 2, 88
Self-sufficiency, 30, 31, 33
Sells, L., 68, 98
Serbin, L. A., 10, 19, 20, 21, 39, 89, 90, 91, 94
Sesame Street, 9
Sewell, W. H., 44, 95
Sex role: attitudes, 32; behavior, 4, 13-17, 78; distinguishing, 4, 5-11; and education, 31; and ethnicity, 27-28; family constellation and, 34; identification, 4, 5; preference, 4, 11-13; situationally specific, 33; and social class, 25-27, 32
Sexuality, 46
Shah, V. P., 44, 95
Sheldon, E. B., 84, 96, 98, 100
Sherman, J. A., 42, 43, 70, 95, 98
Shields, S. A., 65n
Shortell, J. R., 21
Simpson, M. S., 89
Slaby, R. G., 91
Slater, P., 78
Smith, S., 89
Social class, 25-27, 44, 47
Social learning theory, 81
Spatial perception, 42, 43
Stack, C. B., 29, 30, 32, 33, 92
Sternglanz, S. H., 10, 89
Strodbeck, F., 28, 92
Success, 76, 79, 85; fear of, 59-61, 83

Tangri, S., 60n
Tavris, C., 60, 88, 97
Teacher, 39-41, 72-73, 83; attention, 19-20; expectations of, 70-71; male, 54
Television, 9-11, 83
Terminal year, 46-47, 48

Test, 36-37, 41
Thomas, T., 93
Thompson, G. C., 39, 94
Tittle, C. K., 36, 37, 38, 94
Tobias, S., 47, 70, 71, 74n, 81, 85, 96, 99, 100
Tolnick, I. J., 90
Tomboy, 14, 16, 26
Touch, 3
Toy, 15-16; sex-typed, 4, 12, 26
Tracking system, 37-38, 43
Training, 18-19
Tresemer, D., 60, 61, 97
Turner, B. F., 93
Turner, C. B., 93
Tyler, L. E., 91

Unidimensional fallacy, 81
U.S. Department of Health, Education, and Welfare, 38, 39
U.S. Department of Labor, 96

Van Dusen, R. A., 84, 96, 98, 100

Verbal ability, 3
Verbal aggression, 22
Verbal perception, 42
Vicarious gratification, 85-86
Volunteer work, 75, 86

Ward, W. D., 16, 90
Weisstein, N., 76n
Weitzman, L. J., 7, 8, 36, 70, 88, 94, 99
Welfare system, 30
Whitehead, A. N., 43
Whiting, B., xi
Whitney, F. E., 85, 100, 101
Will, J., 2, 88
Wolfle, D., 96
Woman: black, 28-34, 44; college graduate, 56; divorced, 84-85; high achieving, 75-86; "new," 54; reentry, 84-85; role of, 11
Women's movement, 49, 50

Zborowski, M., x
Zook, E. A., 12, 89

LIBRARY OF MOUNT ST. MARY'S COLLEGE EMMITSBURG, MARYLAND

APR 1 4 1983